GET CONSCIOUS

How to Stop Overthinking and Come Alive

ALI WALKER PhD

HAY HOUSE

Carlsbad, California • New York City • London
Sydney •Johannesburg • Vancouver • New Delhi

First published and distributed in the United Kingdom by:
Hay House UK Ltd, Astley House, 33 Notting Hill Gate, London W11 3JQ
Tel: +44 (0)20 3675 2450; Fax: +44 (0)20 3675 2451; www.hayhouse.co.uk

Published and distributed in Australia by:
Hay House Australia Ltd, 18/36 Ralph St, Alexandria NSW 2015
Tel: (61) 2 9669 4299; Fax: (61) 2 9669 4144; www.hayhouse.com.au

Published and distributed in the United States of America by:
Hay House Inc., PO Box 5100, Carlsbad, CA 92018-5100
Tel: (1) 760 431 7695 or (800) 654 5126
Fax: (1) 760 431 6948 or (800) 650 5115; www.hayhouse.com

Published and distributed in the Republic of South Africa by:
Hay House SA (Pty) Ltd, PO Box 990, Witkoppen 2068
info@hayhouse.co.za; www.hayhouse.co.za

Published and distributed in India by:
Hay House Publishers India, Muskaan Complex, Plot No.3, B-2,
Vasant Kunj, New Delhi 110 070
Tel: (91) 11 4176 1620; Fax: (91) 11 4176 1630; www.hayhouse.co.in

Distributed in Canada by:
Raincoast Books, 2440 Viking Way, Richmond, B.C. V6V 1N2
Tel: (1) 604 448 7100; Fax: (1) 604 270 7161; www.raincoast.com

Copyright © 2017 by Ali Walker

Design by Rhett Nacson; Typeset by Bookhouse, Sydney;
Edited by Margie Tubbs

The moral rights of the author have been asserted.

The information given in this book should not be treated as a substitute for professional medical advice; always consult a medical practitioner. Any use of information in this book is at the reader's discretion and risk. Neither the author nor the publisher can be held responsible for any loss, claim or damage arising out of the use, or misuse, of the suggestions made, the failure to take medical advice or for any material on third party websites.

A catalogue record for this book is available from the British Library.

ISBN: 978-1-78180-945-7

Printed in the UK by TJ International Ltd, Padstow, Cornwall.

dedicated to Al,
the love of my life

Contents

Part 2 A Guide to the Four Elements of Conscious Awareness

ELEMENT 1 FEEL

ELEMENT 2 THINK

ELEMENT 3 SENSE

ELEMENT 4 ACT

Reflections

PROLOGUE

Mirage

There is a common tale told by people who have walked in
*   the desert.*
As they struggle along under the scorching sun, they lift
*   their head and gaze into the distance.*
Out of nowhere, a sparkling pool of water suddenly appears.
They blink and refocus.
It's still there: a shimmering oasis.
They rush towards the water, already imagining the cool
*   relief washing over their face and body.*
As they approach, the pool vanishes.
They stop and stare, waiting for it to reappear.
They shake their heads in disbelief, wondering how
*   something so real could suddenly be gone.*
It's a mirage.
The water is an optical illusion, a trick of the light.

We all chase mirages.
Some seduce us for a lifetime.

INTRODUCTION

ANCIENT MIRAGE

The Edge of the World

☐ Leda was an orphan who lived in Greece two and a half thousand years ago. Every morning she would wake with the sunrise and stare at the horizon, believing it to be the edge of the world.

After two years of watching each sunrise and sunset, Leda decided to travel to the horizon to look over the edge. She set out at dawn one morning and walked for hours.

The horizon never seemed to draw nearer.

At the end of the first day, Leda realised that the journey was going to take longer than she thought, so she stopped to stay overnight at an inn. The next morning, she awoke, ate and began walking again.

Days turned into nights. Weeks passed. The landscape changed, but the horizon never came closer. Leda worked along the way, helping at inns and on farms, paying for her food and board.

One day, after reaching the coastline, Leda decided that the way to the edge of the world must be across the water. She secretly boarded a fishing boat. She was discovered in a matter of hours and was forced to work to remain on board. They sailed for days and came no closer. The fishermen called her crazy. They said she had a death wish to want to go near the edge. Even though the boat travelled far from the coast, the edge of the world kept eluding her.

Still, she did not lose faith. Surely her eyes and the sun could not deceive her? When the boat returned to the dock, she started walking along the coast.

On her way to the horizon she had dangerous encounters with violent men and wild animals and was injured more than once. She met different people and learnt many things on her quest. Yet she never savoured these experiences; her only desire was to find the edge of the world.

There was one particular man that she met on her travels. He was different. He was special. He asked her about her quest and she told him what she had set out to do. He declared that he loved her, and that he would accompany her to the edge of the world. He became her companion. They walked and then sailed together towards the horizon, only stopping to eat, work and sleep. They earned enough money to eventually buy their own boat. Occasionally they found a town that they loved and they considered staying on, but they could never really settle on their way to the edge of the world.

During one of their stays in a coastal Greek town, Leda became pregnant. Even this did not stop their journey. They kept sailing on and on until the child—a son—was born. Then they kept sailing until he could eventually steer the boat alongside them. He was raised on the sea.

Many years later, Leda and her husband became weary. They could no longer continue their quest, and they had not yet met anyone who had actually made it to the edge. They decided to stop with the mystery of the horizon still alive in their hearts.

Their son kept sailing towards the edge, with a family of his own.

One day, the son returned to his mother's side as she lay on her deathbed. Between laboured breaths, she whispered: 'My son, I have finally reached the edge of the world. Let me tell you the three things I have discovered:

> **Sometimes what we wholeheartedly believe to be real is an illusion.**
> **We can miss out on our entire lives because we are always searching for something more.**
> **And we pass on our unfinished dreams to the ones we leave behind.**

I can finally see. Don't let the illusions and unfinished dreams of my life determine the course of yours.'

MODERN MIRAGE

The Search for Happiness

☐ When my beautiful grandpa was alive, he often told me the story of his friend, the lawyer. This lawyer was very successful. Like many people, he believed that happiness would be the result of hard work and the wealth that came along with it.

He was determined to climb the ladder in his profession. He started as a paralegal, while he was studying law. After graduating, he spent some years as a lawyer. Then he left the firm to become a barrister (an expert litigator). He enjoyed success as a barrister for many years and was eventually appointed as a Queen's Counsel—an elite group of barristers chosen by the government. After several years as a Queen's Counsel, he became a judge. He spent over a decade as a judge and over the years became very wealthy.

After he had retired, he was talking one day to my grandpa. He lamented that, despite his hard work and external success, he never felt as if he had 'made it.' He was searching for something in his success, but had never found it. He always thought he would discover happiness in his next achievement or in the next phase of his life.

His final reflection was: 'You never arrive.'

The research tells us that his story is universal: when we look for happiness in the future, in our money, in our stuff, in the chase or in the thrill of the deal, we never arrive. In fact, a study by economists from Princeton University in 2010 showed that, once we earn an average annual income, our happiness does not increase by earning more money. This means that if we are comfortable financially and our needs are met, **more money does not increase our life satisfaction**. Another famous study in 1978 by Northwestern University and the University of Massachusetts reported that, when people experience unexpected luck (like winning the lottery) or unexpected tragedy (like a catastrophic car accident), their level of happiness eventually returns to the same level it was prior to the event.

The truth is, while most of us feel 'happy' for some part of each day, achieving happiness in life can be like chasing the horizon. It is always there in moments when we have a higher perspective and yet, when we chase after it and try to catch it, it disappears into thin air. It is always just out of reach—our modern mirage.

So if happiness is not in money, luck or the future, where is it? Where is that purposeful, on track, meaningful, satisfied, joyful feeling of 'arriving' that we are all searching for?

I have been researching this question for several years, and here is what I've discovered . . .

1. Our brains can't make us happy

The human brain, left to its own devices, is unable to make us happy. The human brain is simply a signalling machine that is built to keep us alive and avoid pain. That's it. Most of us are just living according to the programs of our childhood that were installed by our genetics and environment. I call them 'someone like me' programs. For example:

+ This is how much money someone like me earns.
+ This is the kind of relationship someone like me deserves.
+ This is the job someone like me performs.
+ This is when someone like me gets married and has children.

Who is 'someone like me'? Someone from my family, my community, my age, my gender and my country. If you're not happy and living to your highest potential, it's because your brain (a pre-programmed signalling machine) is running your life based on the programs of your past, and the people around you.

2. Life is a series of tiny choices

We have been conditioned to believe that our life and our happiness are defined by our big choices: where we live, our career path, our life partner. In actual fact, our life and our happiness are defined by the tiny choices that we make in each moment about how to think and feel. These tiny choices create momentum; they create a trajectory, as though we are constructing train tracks, and each thought or emotion we have places another track in front of us. It doesn't feel like a big deal to us at the time, but each new track determines our ultimate path and direction.

To live a life that brings us happiness, we must go beyond our brain and live from a different place: our consciousness. Put simply, consciousness is the mind's capacity to direct our awareness and attention. Just like the airport has a control tower that watches and coordinates all of the flights, our mind has a control tower that can watch and coordinate our thoughts, emotions and behaviour. We just need to find the way into the control tower of our mind. We do this by developing our conscious awareness. Conscious awareness exists on a spectrum; at one end of the spectrum, we can be barely conscious after waking from an operation, or semi-conscious after waking in the night. At the other end of the spectrum, we can be extremely alert, calm, open and highly attuned.

This book is about training our minds to be highly conscious. When we are aware of our patterns, our stories, our habits and our desires, we have the power to change them. We have the power to be intentional and perceptive about our life choices. This is **conscious awareness**: the ability to transcend our automatic brain and live with heightened awareness. The more 'conscious' we are, the more we are able to actively choose what to focus on.

So here's my message: **Don't try to be happy, try to be conscious. This will make you happy.**

How to get conscious

In every moment, we have four choices: how to feel, how to think, how to sense and how to act. Here are four steps to enhance your conscious awareness:

Step 1: **Feel** Honour all of your emotions.

Step 2: **Think** Choose only positive thoughts and learn how to direct your brain.

Step 3: **Sense** Trust your senses and the messages of your body.

Step 4: **Act** Work with the flow of life and love.

Happiness comes from practising these four steps every day. If you practise conscious awareness, your outside life will flourish. You will succeed. You will be abundant. You will be surrounded by love. You will arrive. And you will reach the edge of the world.

Here's how I made my way to the edge.

PART 1 LAWYER to LIGHT

CHAPTER 1

Thinkaholic

☐ As children, we all imagine what our lives will look like when we 'grow up'. We create stories of where we might live, what we will do and who we will love. The four-year-old me had very practical ambitions for my adult life: on Monday and Tuesday I would be Superwoman; on Wednesday, Thursday and Friday I would be a mum; and on the weekends I would be a rock star. I had a wide repertoire of two songs: *Walkin' on Sunshine* by Katrina and the Waves and *Live it Up* by Mental as Anything. I would dance around, singing with a brush as a microphone and wearing sunglasses in the shape of stars. I played guitar on my dad's squash racquet.

My dreams changed when I became a very sophisticated eleven-year-old. Of course by then I had all the answers. I was savvy. At eleven, I decided that happiness would come from being a successful lawyer. In preparation for my new life, I tried on my mother's high heels and practised holding a briefcase and car phone. I watched *L.A. Law* and *Law and Order*. I imagined one day driving a bright red convertible, my hair streaming in the breeze. This would be my ultimate declaration of success.

This was my simple fast track to happiness: a brilliant career, airports, a phone and a fast, shiny car. I assumed that, if life looked good on the outside, a positive experience on the inside would follow. So I made it my mission to do as much as I could. Doing was happiness! Achieving would lead to good feelings! If the outside world valued me, then I was on track! And so, without even realising it, I made a choice to silence my authentic, questioning, curious, creative self, and I made up a self that would be acceptable to the world. I was culturally conditioned.

As time went on, I developed a pattern of behaviour that was based on the expectations of people around me. I tried to be a perfect daughter, granddaughter, sister, friend, student, and then employee, wife and mother. I became defined by my dedication to the family, the school, the university, and then the organisation. Living to please others required constant monitoring: I was never relaxed or in the moment. I felt out of control because I was reacting to the external circumstances of my life, rather than creating a life of my own.

This turned me into an over-thinker. Of course I thought too much! I had to keep on top of this 'false me' that I was presenting to the world. I could never switch off my mind, and I was often overwhelmed by my thoughts. Instead of making peace with the chaos in my head, instead of gently taming it, instead of learning to love and understand it, I let it control me.

With my supreme mastery of over-thinking, I gradually became a **thinkaholic**. Unnecessary analysis and complication were my addiction, accompanied by hyperactivity to keep my brain occupied. I studied and worked long hours. I exercised. I filled every spare moment I had catching up with friends or flicking through my phone. I was either worrying about the past or anticipating the future. In my head, there was always a background reason or drama for why I felt dissatisfied: *I can't believe they did that; I'm so busy; I'm so tired; That person can't drive!; It's too noisy; This coffee isn't very good; My job is so boring; It's too cold;* and *Can you believe this guy?* If there was no immediate reason, then I would create one.

Distractions were fuel for my thinkaholic. I always had an underlying feeling of needing to be anywhere other than 'here', other than the moment. I was convinced that the key to my happiness was always somewhere other than where I was: in another relationship, another job, another achievement, another conversation, another city, another country, another hairstyle, another beach, another cafe, another drink, another outfit, another movie . . . anywhere other than inside me.

Here are the five warning signs of a thinkaholic:

1. Usually diverted and distracted from the present moment.
2. Spends most of the time dwelling on the past or speculating about the future.
3. Often finds reasons to create a tangent of new thoughts or a catastrophe out of calm.
4. Often creates a different mental reality or mood, disconnected from what is actually going on.
5. Overanalyses reality to the point of losing touch with authentic emotions and sensations.

Isn't this normal? Isn't this just 'life'?

In the midst of my mental chaos, I searched for my great love. I yearned for a kindred spirit, but instead I had relationships that resembled rollercoaster rides: they were volatile and jarring; exciting then desolate; high then low;

controlling then abandoning; intimate then hurtful; connected then emotionally distant; and smooth sailing then freefalling. I stayed in relationships for too long, simply because they looked good from the outside and because I didn't want to be alone with my thoughts. Of course, I worked out much later that my relationships were just mirrors of my mind. I was looking for the love of my life, but what I found were men who were lost—just like me—on a frantic search with no map.

My non-stop mental traffic would bombard me, affect my moods and make me feel emotionally heavy and drained. My mind was working against me. Even though I was working towards everything I supposedly wanted, I was living unconsciously. I was effectively mindless, running on pre-prepared mental programs based on 'someone like me'. I was so attached to my small world of thoughts and emotions, I couldn't see the entire universe that lay outside.

In the meantime, I started studying law and politics at university. I still thought that this would make me happy.

CHAPTER 2

A New Idea Beckons

☐ In my early twenties, I travelled an hour each way to university, three days a week. My undergraduate studies lasted for five years. During my two-hour commute, I would listen to audio books about depth psychology, positive psychology, philosophy of the mind and archetypes. Even though I was studying law and politics, I was brought to life by philosophy, psychology and the mind. Consciousness became my secret passion.

I expanded my Arts major, so I could study philosophy and sociology. I wanted to understand the relationship between the mind and the world. I fell head over heels in love with the work of Lao Tzu, Socrates, Plato, Plotinus, Aristotle, Immanuel Kant and Georg Wilhelm Friedrich Hegel. Then I discovered the depth psychologists: Carl Jung, Sigmund Freud and Hannah Arendt. This led me into the mystics, healers and poets.

These thinkers connected me to a deeper awareness of myself. It was like turning back to a long-forgotten inner world where I felt most at home. They lifted the veil on a new dimension of existence and gave me my first real insight into the part of me beyond my thoughts. They made me wonder whether my mind might actually be a source of hidden treasure. For the first time, my thinkaholic was silenced.

I have to tell you how powerful this was for me. It was like I was being tapped on the shoulder by some force, insisting that I connect with these new ideas. It whispered in my ear, promising to change my life.

After being transformed by these revelations, I would arrive at my law and politics classes and learn all about society, culture and the constitution. I was learning alongside people who were top academic performers: articulate, hardworking, ambitious and clever. This competition brought me back into my thinkaholic, back into the race. It felt like I was living a double life, and I guess I was. The tension between my thinkaholic and my consciousness began. I had a foot in two worlds.

After I graduated from my undergraduate degrees, I took some time off to figure out what I wanted to do. I started a business called *Open Your Eyes*, giving seminars in high schools about self-worth, feminism and distorted images of women in the media. I rediscovered my love of music and singing. I went travelling around Europe. That four-year-old started to hope that she might have a place in my life after all!

While I loved the freedom of post-university life, I always felt that something was missing. I persistently felt too floaty, fickle, capricious or 'not enough.' I had changed the outer circumstances of my life, but I had still taken my fears with me. I still wasn't happy. Regardless of what I did, I never felt as if I had arrived. I didn't feel whole. Even though I loved hanging out in this new territory, it didn't yet have a firm enough foundation for me to live on. I still didn't realise that **it's not about what you do.**

So I returned to familiar territory and followed the instructions of my thinkaholic. I applied for a 'real job' working as a criminal lawyer.

CHAPTER 3

The Lawyer in theSuit

☐ I became the lawyer. I wore the suits. I was a fully-fledged adult, participating in the world. On my first day, I was allocated a desk and left alone with two folders of material to prepare for a trial. I had to send out subpoenas for witnesses, brief the prosecutor, interview the victims, and put together a detailed timeline of the offence. The trial was for an aggravated robbery. There were photos. My eyes widened and my heart skipped a beat. They were graphic, bloody photos of a violent robbery— and I was shocked and disturbed.

What had I expected? I was a criminal lawyer! Perhaps in a way I was still that eleven-year-old in my head, expecting the *LA Law* montage version of law, with synthesiser music in the background.

A few months into the job, I began to realise that violent robberies were the easy cases. They were the ones I hoped for. It was sexual assaults that brought me undone, especially the child sexual assaults.

A series of heartbreaking events changed the way I saw the world forever. The first was a pre-trial meeting with a victim of child sexual assault. Now in her twenties, this woman was giving evidence against a man who had sexually assaulted her when she was a girl. As she recounted the evidence in her statement, she began to cry. She was reliving a time in her life that would traumatise her forever. I sat there, offering tissues and trying to be as helpful as I could, tears welling in my eyes. Yet my job was not to comfort her. If she didn't deliver all of her evidence, we wouldn't get a conviction. I looked at the prosecutor, who seemed unshakeable and so sure of her role in the process. I wasn't sure I could end up like that. Heartbreak number one.

The second heartbreak happened after the trial began. Every morning for several weeks, we would arrive at the courtroom and the accused would be waiting with his family: his wife in her late teens and their newborn baby. His wife was very sweet. She happily turned up with her baby every day of that trial, almost as if she didn't realise what was going on. Clearly she knew what was happening, but she seemed so cheerful outside the courtroom that it made me wonder if she really understood the repercussions of the trial. She would smile at me and say hello as we all walked in, as if we were filing into a school classroom. She must not have known that I worked for the prosecution, and that our objective was to put her husband in jail for the next twenty years. I would smile back and say hello, as if I were part of a twisted play. Heartbreak number two.

The accused man (her husband) was eventually found guilty of more than thirty counts of child sexual assault. His young wife stopped talking to me, and looked at me as though I had betrayed her. After the verdict was returned and we were back in the office, my colleagues were over the moon that we had won. They were punching the air. I felt sick. Of course I didn't want him to go unpunished for his crimes but, in my mind, the trial still left everything unhealed and simply created another generation of despair.

At the sentencing hearing two weeks later, he finally shared his pain with the courtroom: his own abuse as a child, his subsequent drug addiction, his inability to heal from his abuse and how he had tried to make sense of it by abusing someone else. As I sat at the bar table and dictated a transcript of the hearing, my tears dropped onto the pages. I started to lose faith in the law that had underpinned my years of study. I definitely didn't feel as though justice had been done. Heartbreak number three.

At the same time, I was involved in another trial of sexual assault. In that case, a woman came home from a work party and was raped in her bed by a man who was staying in her apartment. He was a friend of her flatmate.

In the courtroom, he looked so normal. He looked like an average white man in his thirties; a man you would sit next to on a bus. After work that day, I took the bus home and glanced around at the other passengers, wondering whether they had caused deep pain and trauma for anyone. I caught myself thinking the worst of people and started to wonder whether all of us are capable of destruction and evil. The vicarious trauma started to creep in. Heartbreak number four.

Around the same time as these trials, my body started developing symptoms that I had never experienced before. I would organise last minute doctors' appointments in the city and rush off for consultations in my lunch hour. The results of medical tests invariably came back as normal. I was just in the wrong place, and my body knew it. These were the early signals and warning signs from my body to get out of there.

On the day I finally decided to leave my job, I was trapped in the office elevator. I have struggled with claustrophobia since childhood and don't like elevators at the best of times. I was hurrying across to court to hear a verdict and dashed into the elevator with a few of my colleagues. When the doors closed, we pressed the button for the ground floor and nothing happened. For about a minute. And then a minute more. On the verge of a panic attack, I ran to the doors and tried to pry them open. My colleagues asked me if I was okay, and I can't remember what I said. We were only in that elevator for about ten minutes, but it was the last straw for that job.

I realised that the elevator was a symbol for my reality. I was trapped in a place I didn't want to be in. I decided that it wasn't normal to cry regularly because of my job, and that work should not be a source of heartbreak. There are people who feel aligned to this sort of work and I salute them. They carry out an important public service and are good, noble people. I was just made for other things.

My point is this: I was living my childhood dreams, but they were not making me happy. I was trying to be impressive and worthwhile in the world, even though my body and my mind were completely out of balance. My ideals about people and the world were shattering. I was losing my sense of joy.

But there were two surprises on the way: a life-changing man and a life-altering course. All I had to do was take a leap of faith, in the hope that my happiness might be found somewhere else.

CHAPTER 4

New Worlds

☐ Around the time I was questioning my work as a lawyer, I met my future husband. We fell deeply in love. He was, and still is, like a log fire on a cold night: warm, magnetic, comforting, powerful and alluring. When I quit my job, he told me that he didn't care what I did or what I achieved; only who I was. This was a revelation to me, because I certainly didn't feel that way about myself.

My sense of direction was in tatters—where was happiness if I wasn't a lawyer? I decided to go back to university to find out what I really wanted to do. I enrolled in a Masters in International Relations and International Law. For a few weeks between jobs I struggled to pay the rent, but then I started tutoring and lecturing at university in international law, politics and sociology. I loved it. I felt like I had found a home with the experience of teaching, the potential of ideas and the positive energy of the university.

Around this time, my best friend from school, Patrice, finished studying kinesiology. She introduced me to the world of vibrational medicine and subtle energies. Patrice lived on

Scotland Island, off the coast in Pittwater, near Sydney's Northern Beaches. I would often stay over at her place, built like a giant treehouse on the island. She would pick me up in her runabout boat and take me over the water. It was like entering a new world.

Patrice's home was an epicentre of feminine power. She would set up a massage table on the verandah and give energetic healings as the birds chirped in the background. Without talking, I was guided by Patrice to work through the loops and blockages in my mind. This started to unravel my thinkaholic further, as my mind became a familiar and comforting place. I started to feel excited about the potential of the mind, rather than regarding it as a place of chaos and uneasiness. I realised that the mind is not simply confined to the brain: it is the consciousness that surrounds us.

I followed my curiosity and decided to explore some of the ideas about the mind that had captivated me for so many years. I enrolled in a Graduate Diploma in Integral Coaching. The course was described in the syllabus as 'a journey into the artistry of change making and soul care applied to life and work.' I considered it a balance between my everyday demands and the part of me that wanted to ask the bigger questions of life.

My teacher in the Integral Coaching course was a psychologist. He had a background in clinical psychology, counselling and shamanism. In the course, he fused Native American spirituality with coaching psychology and analytical psychology, as developed by Carl Jung. He took me into the world of consciousness—a world I had only ever read about or listened to.

For the first time in my life, I went inside my mind and realised that it was where I felt most at home. The mind that I had buried was actually a place of wonderment and bliss. The darkness, shadows and pressures were just illusions I had created—tricks of the light. They were mirages that ruled my life. I started to experience glimpses of the infinite consciousness I thought were reserved for the mystics and enlightened ones. I realised that higher states of consciousness were for the willing, not just the chosen. It was exhilarating! These were the eternal truths I had been looking for. I learnt to engage with my archetypes. I embraced deep vulnerability and power. This steered me towards a different course and I would never be the same again.

This was my initiation into **consciousness.**

CHAPTER 5

Shamanic Journey

☐ As part of the course I participated in a **shamanic journey**: an ancient practice of guided meditation based on the healing traditions of indigenous peoples throughout the world. It is facilitated by a shaman, traditionally known as a messenger between the human and spirit worlds. The shaman uses the sounds of rattling, drumming and whistling to induce an altered state of perception that allows you to access higher parts of your mind.

My shamanic journey happened on an ordinary day in an ordinary place, but it was one of the most extraordinary experiences I've ever had. A group of students were gathered and our shaman teacher instructed us to lie down on yoga mats and pillows in a large room. As we relaxed onto our mats, he started by saying:

When you hear the beating of the drum your spirit will be taken on a journey. You will become nature and transform into the sky, the air, the soil or the water. You will meet your power animals and they will guide you.

We started with a simple breath meditation to relax our minds. Then the drumming began. The pounding of the constant beat was confronting and yet oddly comforting. I closed my eyes and began to breathe deeply. The repetitious drumming was so intense that I began to feel as though it was happening inside my body. The drumming was then accompanied by rattling sounds. I became aware of my body in a way that I had never contemplated, as though I was consumed by it, and yet observed it at the same time. I heard another, more immediate sound from within the room. I realised that the shaman had started to use rattles. This combination of sounds—the drum beating, my rhythmic breathing and the rattling—was like the earth speaking, singing and crying all at once.

I instinctively felt my body sink into the earth. I felt a strange sensation of tunnelling through soil. I felt as though my body was ploughing through layers of the ground. I felt strangely calm while travelling into the depths of the moist earth.

Suddenly I became aware of a snow leopard raising its head from the grass, as if it was also hearing the rattling. I was disturbed and excited by the prospect of summoning a snow leopard. I had never seen a snow leopard in real life before, but I was certain it was one. It began sprinting towards the rattling sound. I could almost feel the power of its body, as it moved so quickly across the plains. I could make out the rippling muscles in its legs, as it pounded across the grasslands of my imagination.

Suddenly, I found myself in the middle of a rainforest and I slid further down into the earth. I was in a dark cave when I came face to face with my snow leopard. It lunged towards me, baring its teeth, and began to rip away at my flesh, encouraging rebirth and new beginnings. While the idea of being skinned by a leopard was violent and graphic, I surprised myself by surrendering to the process. I had no fear and felt no pain because I just knew that it was necessary, like someone brushing knots out of my hair. I never felt that the leopard was 'attacking' me. It felt natural, like pulling away dead skin and allowing fresh skin to take its place. This type of experience is considered to be part of the healing journey in shamanism.

After the snow leopard had shed my skin, I sank back into the earth and re-emerged on an island beach with fine white sand. The scene was radiant and idyllic. I saw thousands of white butterflies fluttering around me, reminding me to breathe and to be at peace in the moment. I gazed at the tropical foliage, then a rattlesnake slid out from between the trees. Again, I had no fear and simply invited the snake to teach me its lesson. The snake quickly slid towards me. It encircled my bleeding and raw body from my legs to my chest, almost to the point of suffocation. Once again I surrendered to the snake, allowing myself to die in one form, so that I could be reborn in another.

Once my shedding was complete, I lay on the beach. A peacock emerged. The snow leopard and the rattlesnake both had the destruction impulse, whereas the peacock appeared for a different reason. The peacock displayed all his dazzling colours, flaring his feathers towards me and silently teaching me to honour and celebrate my mind without judgement. The peacock turned and asked me: 'Does anyone judge the peacock when he proudly displays his feathers? Does the peacock judge himself or his beautiful tail?' I realised that burying my mind was akin to the peacock hiding his tail.

In the next moment, I was catapulted into a tunnel that wound its way into the deep ocean. I tapped into the energy of the sea and witnessed the flourishing marine life before me. In this altered state of perception, being under the sea was the most normal experience in the world. Abruptly, a shark tried to make contact with me on my left side, inviting me to unite with his energy. I resisted at first, instinctively fearing attack. Then to my right a baby dolphin appeared, vulnerable and defenceless. Both the shark and the dolphin beckoned me to join them. I felt that, if I gravitated towards the dolphin, we would both be unprotected and liable to attack by the shark. Yet if I chose the shark, I would be leaving the dolphin on its own and I would become the predator.

In my uncertainty, the shark told me to have no fear and assured me that we have all arranged to meet various predators along the road. We all carry victim and predator energy within us. As long as we connect with our inner victim and our predator, we will stop experiencing predators outside ourselves. These external predators are all illusions. After hearing and understanding this, both the shark and the dolphin dissolved into my body and spirit; they weren't 'outside me' any longer.

I was then drawn back through the tunnel, into the cave and up through the moist earth of the rainforest, back into my body. I became aware of being back in the room. I realised that the rattling had stopped, but I wasn't sure how long the silence had lasted. I opened my eyes and saw the shaman standing by me.

The shaman spoke: 'Did you meet your power animals?'

I nodded, still blinking and disoriented by the experience.

'Can I blow them into your body?' he asked matter-of-factly.

'Uh, what does that involve?' I asked.

I momentarily felt vulnerable but then remembered the message of the shark: predators are illusions.

The shaman said, 'My purpose is to secure the teachings of the animals into your soul. Blowing them into your body means that I lay my hands over your solar plexus and seal the spirit of your animals with my breath.'

'Okay,' I agreed.

He knelt down next to me. He cupped his hands over my stomach, forming a kind of volcano shape, then lent his face down. He blew and whistled into the hole between his hands, until I could feel his breath through my clothes.

'It is done,' said the shaman.

I was overwhelmed by the profound learning I had received from this shaman and my majestic power animals. It occurred to me that this type of journeying was potentially an answer to the human need for ecstatic escape. Without drinking or ingesting any substances, I had just entered another realm of seeing and being that was wise and deeply healing. I had a heightened experience of being interconnected with every living thing. I realised that there was a part of my mind that was far more powerful than my thoughts.

I went beyond my thoughts and entered a **new dimension of consciousness.**

CHAPTER 6

Vision Quest

One does not become enlightened by imagining figures
of light, but by making the darkness conscious.

CARL JUNG, FOUNDER OF ANALYTICAL PSYCHOLOGY

☐ Shortly after the shamanic journey, I went on a **vision quest**.
A vision quest is a Native American rite of passage, which
involves between one and four days secluded in nature in search
of spiritual purpose. In the modern context, it is a powerful
retreat from day-to-day life that draws out our deepest fears,
in order to transform them into our greatest power.

All of the quest participants travelled to the Blue Mountains
(a couple of hours west of Sydney) for the weekend. Our quest
would involve one full day, from sunrise to sunset, alone in the
heart of the mountains. The only information I had about the
day was this:

> Solitude in nature provides an opportunity to open with
> challenge or trust to the call of Spirit, the wild and the voice
> of the soul, as reflected in nature. In this 'soul threshold'
> experience, transition beyond the mundane daily life demands
> and world into the dreaming process that beckons your release
> into the cultivation of your soul life and vision.

The thinkaholic in me was completely terrified; I would be spending my 26th birthday alone in the bush with no mobile reception. The deeper part of me—my consciousness—was wildly excited.

On the Friday morning, I drove to the Blue Mountains with two of my fellow questers and we settled into the cabins. I was sharing a cabin with a beautiful, nurturing woman in her forties. She had been on vision quests before and became an inspiring guide for the weekend. She even gave me a birthday gift: a bracelet made by indigenous Australian women, which was symbolic of a rite of passage.

The Friday activities were important training for the Saturday quest. According to tradition, vision quests need careful preparation and very clear intent. We shared the purpose for our vision quest with others in the group. We uncovered the patterns that had brought us to this point in our lives. We talked about our transitions and our deep fears that were being evoked by the quest.

At different times, I thought about leaving and going home, but then I hadn't brought my own car. Going off to sleep that night I felt trapped, all alone, with only myself and my thoughts . . . a metaphor for life, I guess.

We all woke well before dawn on the Saturday morning, dressed and had breakfast. For the day, we were given lunch, water, maps, a torch and a box of matches. We were instructed to take whatever we could carry to keep us warm. It was the middle of autumn, and the Blue Mountains can be very cold.

In the darkness before dawn, we all drove to the beginning of a hiking trail. Our instructions were to walk the seven-kilometre hike alone. Along the way, we were to find a place to spend the day: our 'power spot.' The power spot would supposedly stand out to us as a safe and inviting space in nature. This would be the site of our vision quest. We would need to intuitively open up to the messages of nature in finding our spot. Once we located our power spot, we were to stay in that space until we saw that the sun was beginning to fade. At that time, we had to finish the hike and make it to the peak before sunset.

It was still pitch black when we started the hike. As each of us departed on the hike in intervals, the facilitators circled the smoke of sage leaves around us and gave us a blessing. I set off, shaking, down the dark bush track with my torch alight and my senses on high alert. I had tears in my eyes; it was my birthday. I love my birthday. I love celebrating with my friends and family. I had never done anything like this before. I am not a hiker or a bushwalker. I am not 'at home' in the bush. I am at home near the ocean. To me, the bush is daunting and cavernous . . . especially when alone.

This was a symbol for entering the unfamiliar territory in my mind.

To make the whole situation a bit more confronting, the hike they had chosen for us went down to the bottom of a valley. The track wound into the dark valley in spirals. I wouldn't see another person for approximately eight to ten hours. All of my fearful thoughts became louder and louder. My heart was racing.

And then I came to a part of the track where it was unclear which way I should go. There were no signs. I was convinced I had come the wrong way. I panicked. I turned around and started to run back up the hill, back to the cars, back to people, back to control, back to safety. After running uphill for about 100 metres, I ran into one of my fellow questers.

'What's wrong?' he asked, clearly seeing the fear on my face.

'I went the wrong way,' I spluttered. 'I got lost.'

'This is the way,' he answered gently. 'You're going to be okay.'

His soothing voice calmed me down enough to realise that I actually did want to do this. I wanted to finish the quest. I took a deep breath and nodded.

'Okay,' he said. 'You go first. I'll wait here for a while and then I'll come after.'

Just the thought that someone would be following me was reassuring, even if I wouldn't see him for the rest of the day. Deep down, I knew I had to do this. If I didn't carry out my quest, these same fears could resurface again in my life—but with a different face.

I turned around and set off again, determined to undertake the quest. These fears of life and the unknown (of being alone and completely self-sufficient) were always taunting me from the sidelines. I needed to confront them head-on. My higher consciousness urged me to go forward. So I made my way down the slippery valley, into the guts of the earth, in the hazy darkness just before dawn. In my uncertainty, I called on something outside me to help me get to the end.

I continued on and the sun eventually started to shed light on the verdant valley. I started to relax as I realised the unknown was not going to kill me. It became a magical and humbling experience to be alone in the midst of nature's wonders.

I began to sense around for power spots. I was nervous about this . . . what if I didn't get a power spot feeling? What if I just kept wandering and couldn't find my place? I began to realise why this quest was so important: it basically revealed all of my fears about life. It wasn't a fear of being alone in the bush. It was a fear of losing control, of being out of my comfort zone and not finding my place in the world. After an hour or so of walking, I saw a little raised area under a small cliff to one side of the track. It felt right. It was close enough to the track not to get lost, but far enough away so I wouldn't be seen by any hikers throughout the day.

I made my way to the spot and became comfortable. I made a blanket out of my jacket and a pillow out of my backpack. I settled in and fell asleep. When I woke up it was eight o'clock. Eight more hours to go. In one spot.

The hours passed, some quickly and others slowly. I wrote in my journal. I sat and meditated. A few times, I tried to jump up and down with my phone in order to get reception. The funny thing about fears is that when you face them, they become so ordinary. The solitude in nature was healing, confronting and ordinary at the same time. I was still me, just in a different setting.

Around 4pm, the sun began to set so I gathered up my things and made my way back to the track. I scanned my map and estimated that it would take me just under two hours to get back—I had five kilometres to go. The track was often unmarked and sometimes I had to guess which direction to take. There were some tricky moments and the last kilometre was completely uphill, but the feeling that I had when I reached the top was incredible. I felt invincible. It was like no other feeling I've ever had. I was victorious! I had faced my vulnerability and embraced my power. No awards or achievements in my life have come close.

I had experienced **the power of consciousness.**

CHAPTER $\boxed{7}$

The PhD

☐ Throughout these extraordinary experiences, I became even more fascinated with the mind and consciousness. How was I able to access these powerful hidden compartments in my mind simply through an energetic healing, a guided meditation and spending time alone in nature? I wanted to understand more about the mind's potential.

Yet at that time, I still believed that only my thinkaholic knew how to look after me, to ground my identity and connect me to real life. I thought the world had to define my path. I worked hard at my Masters in International Law, and taught ten classes a week at university with 250 students. I became used to my split life, using my thinkaholic for working and relating to the external world and my higher consciousness for relating to my self and my inner world. My inner and outer worlds were so intertwined and yet so distant. It was as though I had split in two.

After my coaching course had ended and my Masters year was over, I decided to undertake a PhD in consciousness. This was my way of bringing the two worlds together. I was fortunate to have a scholarship at the Australian National University that paid me to conduct my research, which meant that I could support myself as I embarked upon this adventure into the nature of mind. The PhD started out as a way to research the nature of individual and collective consciousness. This independent research seemed like a haven for me to figure out where I needed to go. I thought I would do my PhD day-to-day, and in my spare time I would access higher modes of being.

But what is a PhD? It's a lot of time spent alone, absorbed in research materials. Three and a half years to be precise. And what was my PhD on? Ideas about consciousness and psychology applied to law and culture. I was trying to integrate my learning, and I was trying to unite my thinker and my consciousness.

I immersed myself in research on the ego, persona, unconscious material, archetypes and the shadow. I analysed a variety of perspectives on the concept of consciousness, including neuroscience, psychology, philosophy, sociology and social psychology. I travelled to the US to research with Alexander Wendt, Professor of International Security, who explores the connection between social science and quantum mechanics. He talked about the world as a hologram and the role for consciousness from the quantum perspective. I presented at conferences around the world.

I was beginning to see consciousness as not just an idea but as the background of our **entire human experience.**

Even experts who have been studying consciousness for decades can't agree on what it is, or where it is located. All we know is that humans have the unique ability to both inhabit our minds and observe them. We experience life, and we watch ourselves doing it. Why? How?

Here's how I think of the difference between the brain, the mind and consciousness. Our brains are like the physical space of an airport, where flights constantly take off and land. The flights are the thoughts, emotions and sensations that are generated in our brain. Coming and going, nonstop, until we fall asleep, during which time there is still low-level activity going on, just like the airport in the middle of the night. The brain, like the airport, is just an objective site for a lot of activity to take place.

The mind is like the subjective experience of the airport and the unique way it operates. The mind of the airport is the way that all the parts interact and coordinate. The mind encompasses the gates, the departure lounges, the security and the baggage claim across all the terminals. The mind is how the airport works.

Consciousness is the higher intelligence—the control tower—directing the flight timing and activity. Consciousness controls the focus and attention of the brain and mind. When we enter the control tower, we see that our brains and minds are actually malleable and obey the commands of our consciousness. As we increasingly cultivate the conscious observer, the brain becomes the servant and consciousness becomes the master.

Another way to think of the relationship between the brain, the mind and consciousness is by using a video game. The brain is the game device and hardware. The mind is the character in the game that simply follows commands, yet has its own internal experience. Consciousness is the person playing the game and directing the activity. If you stop pressing the buttons, the character in the game stops moving. The brain is the device, the mind is the character and consciousness is the person holding the game controller.

In the case of both the airport and the video game, there is another entity or network directing the activity. Our consciousness is the higher intelligence directing our mental activity. We often direct our brains without realising it. When we want to be more alert, we have caffeine and our heart beats faster. When we want to be more relaxed, we might have alcohol or we close our eyes and breathe deeply. If I consciously choose to meditate, I am directing the activity of my brain. If I consciously choose to hug someone, I am directing the activity of my brain. The brain will respond physiologically with hormones, chemicals and neurotransmitters. The mind will respond with thoughts, emotions and sensations. Our consciousness is the antenna or remote control for our mind.

Theory became practice, as I discovered that the brain is changeable and responsive to the commands of conscious awareness. I discovered that **my consciousness actually controls my thinker.**

CHAPTER 8

Remembering My Selves

☐ During my PhD I started practising daily meditation, as I became familiar with the research on its transformative potential. I also used creative writing and journaling as a way to relax and balance out the formality of academic writing. Journaling is the daily practice of recording thoughts, in order to navigate the different parts of the mind. In my case, the journaling often began with the mundane aspects of my life and became more in-depth as I progressed. In this way, my writing became a window into another world.

One night, towards the end of my PhD, I started to write in my journal and the words took on a life of their own. My writing was flowing and I was freely expressing myself. After writing for some time, I slowly began to see patterns emerging in the words—it was like some phrases and paragraphs were being written by one part of me, while other words were from another part altogether. Every so often, the language would shift and I would start writing from a completely different perspective.

Suddenly, something occurred to me. I stopped writing. I gathered up a pile of my old journals and started to flick through them. As I read my words from over the years, I could see the same thoughts and emotions repeated throughout the pages. I started making sense of the patterns and I could see that there were many different parts of me all vying for a voice in my decisions. They all had distinct voices.

For the first time in my life, I consciously decided to acknowledge the parts and actually give them all awareness and attention. I allowed them space to reveal themselves and their voices. I used a technique called 'voice dialogue', created by Hal and Sidra Stone. The Stones pioneered this approach in 1972, based on the idea that we are not one but many selves. Each of our 'selves' or 'sub-personalities' affects our choices and how we see the world.

In my writing, my different selves began to reveal themselves to me. There was a scholar who often becomes so engrossed in learning that she forgets to eat and shower. I recognised her as the part of me that gets so distracted by work that I trip over the computer cord at 11pm and find stray peas in my dressing-gown pocket as I clean my teeth before bed. There was another self: a passionate teacher who longs to share her message with the world. She is the part of me that shows up for my weekly radio segment and teaches courses at uni. There was a down-to-earth woman, faithfully devoted to her partner, family and friends (she makes the bed, changes the nappies, breastfeeds, does the washing and loves chatting on the phone). There was a stick-thin woman who writes in cafes, has long conversations about philosophy and wears black leather boots. She would like to live alone in a small but chic apartment (as you can imagine, the mother and the philosopher don't often agree on much). And then a barefoot bohemian materialised, who'd like to be a travelling folk singer. Behind them all, seated in the dark, was a priestess who is brought to life by eternal truths. She urges me to dedicate myself to the path of consciousness.

These were the strands of me that I recognised, and I could tie them to significant life decisions I had made. I could imagine their faces, their voices, their ages and how they would dress.

Then the subversive shadow voices started to emerge: a judgemental critic (looking like a Pilgrim, fresh off the *Mayflower*); a hyper-vigilant victim and martyr (who often hang out together in the shadows); a carefree and iconoclastic artist; a femme fatale who has no intention of ever settling down and fantasises about escaping her life; an innocent yet anxious inner child, who just wants to sing and spend all day at the beach; an insecure teenager with braces, who likes playing netball but is riddled with self-doubt; an undermining, melancholic saboteur as well as many others (including some that cannot even be named yet, because they lurk in the deep, dark shadows). These were the parts of me that I repeatedly attracted in the outside world as my unhealed elements.

The patterns that I uncovered were my inner selves, with individual strengths, weaknesses, moods, preferences, areas of expertise and vulnerabilities. They were unique voices with their own stories and identities. They even felt different, once I gave them space and embodied them. Each self had her own mythologies and stories to light her path. I knew that they were alive in me, as my inner voices. I immediately understood that all of my selves occupy territory in my mind—they are all of the parts that need to be consulted when I am making decisions. In one way I am aligned with them; in another way they have a life of their own. This experience brought archetypes to life for me. My selves were directing the course of my life.

Later that night, my husband came home from work and sat down next to me on the couch to fill me in on his day. He started to talk about one of his businesses. I was listening to him speak, and occasionally asking questions. After about fifteen minutes, I started to see that my husband's 'real world' conflict was actually arising from a conflict between two of his selves.

As he spoke, I started to identify the two selves. It was as though a light was switched on inside his mind, and I became aware of different parts of him coming to life. It was like my husband had split into two different men. His inner selves were revealing themselves in everyday conversation. I was listening to two people having a conversation, except the people were two selves that were parts of my husband's consciousness.

I specifically identified two selves conflicting on their attitude to his businesses: a hard worker and an entrepreneur. Every time my husband went back and forth between the two parts of him, I could see that he subtly shifted his sitting position, transformed his facial expressions and mannerisms, changed the tone of his voice and used different language. I could intuitively hear different patterns in his speech, as if he were embodying different people. One part of him (his hard worker self) was seeing the solution as needing to put his head down, get up earlier, work harder and put in more hours. He would say this vehemently—but then he would shift into another part (his entrepreneur) and see the solution as him needing to tweak the business to make it more profitable. The entrepreneur wanted him to work smarter, not harder. He called on him to build the business through innovative strategy. I could see his different 'selves' take over his mind and body whenever he spoke. I offered these selves to him and he found them helpful to visualise.

This was my first realisation that the contents of our mind (our selves, our fears and our thought patterns) have a fundamental impact on the practical details of our lives. We cannot split our day-to-day life from the inner workings of our mind. In fact, a 'real world' problem is often the result of an 'inner world' conflict. Here was my husband with a very real issue in his business and the answer was found in his selves. To this day, whenever he needs business advice, he draws on the insights of these two selves and arrives at the solution he needs. The outer details of our lives are simply a reflection of the interactions within our minds.

Consciousness took on a new power for me.

My PhD research combined with experiences in my personal life brought me to the conclusion that consciousness (in the form of awareness) is the missing link in our collective search for happiness and meaning. I began to formulate **teaching techniques for self-awareness**.

CHAPTER 9

Mindfulness and Mothering

☐ After I finished my PhD, I became a mother for the first time. It goes without saying that motherhood changed me forever. Like all new parents, I went through the shattering defeats of sleep deprivation and the complete loss of autonomy. I felt broken by the responsibility. But my life suddenly took on a new dimension. I was slowly but steadily rebuilt, through the sheer amazement that I could love someone so much. My son and I both fell into our beautiful routine together—monotonous, ecstatic, hideous, sublime, chaotic, sacred, lonely, intimate and always exhausting. In the process of embracing unconditional love, I was made raw to the point where I could only do things that felt natural and nourishing.

No longer could I spend my time overanalysing. I tried, but there simply wasn't time to think too much, and I quickly worked out that there is no such thing as a perfect mother or a perfect child. My baby was now centrestage in my life. The afternoon I was awarded my PhD, I found out over the phone while I was trying to keep my son from jumping into the dryer.

Being with my son every day forced me to confront my thinkaholic; for the first time in my adult life I was left alone with nowhere to channel my (constant) thoughts. Who was I, if I wasn't out achieving in the world? Didn't happiness come from the outside? Where could my thinkaholic go?

My son loved the bedtime story, *We're Going on a Bear Hunt*, by Michael Rosen and Helen Oxenbury. As though the universe itself was communicating with me, I would read him the refrain each night:

> *We can't go over it, we can't go under it. Oh no! We've got to go through it.*

The answer was within. I had to go through it. After hitting many (mental) brick walls, and leaning on my own mother for her eternal goodness and wisdom, I started to get quieter than I had ever been. In order to escape the noise in my mind, I found mindfulness.

I made a mindfulness practice out of cleaning my son's highchair, when he first started eating solid food. He would make a major mess of the highchair every night and I wouldn't have time to clean it immediately, because I would bath him straightaway and then breastfeed and put him down to sleep. Every night after walking out of his room, I would see the dirty highchair and cringe. Cleaning it was the last thing I felt like doing after a long day. For the first month or so I would sigh with exasperation, trudge into the kitchen, grab the cloth, and then spray and clean it as quickly as possible. I wanted to fast forward through this boring task, so I could relax on the couch.

After weeks of this routine, I realised that I brought this fast-forward attitude to so many moments in my day: when filling my car with petrol, cleaning my teeth, making my bed, blow-drying my hair or driving, I was effectively pressing the fast-forward button in my head. I was simply waiting for these moments to pass, because I had deemed them boring, second-class moments of my life. Parenthood had brought along so many chores that I resented (changing nappies, making purees, cleaning up toys and washing, just to name a few). I came to the point one day where I realised that I could fast forward through my entire life, if I only chose to be present for moments I judged as particularly fun or happy.

When I started training my brain to find flow in each moment, I saw the dirty highchair as my mindfulness practice: it was an opportunity to surrender with non-judgement to whatever life handed me. When I brought mindfulness to the moment, cleaning the highchair had the same effect on me as if I was already relaxing on the couch watching my favourite TV series. This was mind training: if I treated the dirty highchair as a relaxing task, then it was. I just had to repackage my associations with relaxing. Aha! I was in control of my mind and my thoughts. I just had to practise it.

When my second son was born three years later, I surprised myself by being much more accepting of whatever came my way. I had no expectations of him or of me, so I was able to allow whatever the moment presented. Then, I could let the love in.

This was mindfulness expanding into heartfulness. And this was something I wrote at that time:

The Key

I am waking up to a land I've always known,
But never knew was here.
I am waking up to a dream I've only witnessed
With my eyes closed.
The key was in my pocket.
It opened treasure I had stored away.
If I do nothing else,
I found you, I found you.
The fire, the words and the song
They all needed me to be real.
I'll rise and see that you are all of me,
I found you, I found you.

The only way I was going to live the life I imagined was to use my consciousness as my guide. I had to accept that I was living on the rollercoaster of life, and all I could do was change my experience of that rollercoaster. At each twist and turn of the ride, I had to transcend the thinker and live from my conscious awareness. I had to replace the worry, anxiety, overanalysis and fast forwarding of the thinker with the gratitude, abundance, mindfulness, wonder and joy of consciousness.

It's the same story for every person who learns to be happy. Happiness is a habit and a skill—not a perfect life. Happy people have wonderful lives simply because they see them that way.

CHAPTER 10

Teaching Awareness

What you seek is seeking you.

RUMI, POET AND SUFI MYSTIC

☐ In the years after I became a mother, I continued university teaching and pursued my work as a social researcher. I also started teaching mind training, awareness and mindfulness to individuals and groups. I helped clients navigate the stories and patterns in their consciousness—what I call their 'invisible personality.'

By entering our inner worlds through self-awareness, meditation and mindfulness, we can understand these patterns and maximise the power of our minds. It's like learning a new language: our inner worlds have the power to shape our reality in our outer worlds. Accessing consciousness brings a new kind of meaning-making that can light up our lives.

I have found it effective to develop powerful images to help people bring awareness to their life experiences. During every session, I create impressions and images of consciousness with the people in front of me. The best way to describe it is that while someone is speaking to me, I translate their story in selves, symbols and metaphors. For example, I have a client who is very calm, composed and diplomatic in her daily life. She is a working mother with a demanding job. Many people, including her friends and colleagues, often marvel at how she is able to serenely manage the constant conflict in her work and the chaos of all her responsibilities. We found an inner self in her consciousness in the form of a Chinese martial artist, who constantly practises tai chi in her mind. This allows her to deal with the ongoing conflict in her work in a calm way. She now uses the image as an effective stress reduction tool so that, whenever chaos arises at home or work, she imagines a peaceful Chinese woman dispersing and diffusing energy.

When we open up to our consciousness, we transform from one individual in a body to many selves in a field of consciousness. The places we go in our minds have real consequences for the way we experience our lives. I worked with a teenage girl just out of hospital with anorexia—we identified a flickering candle in her field of consciousness, with no protection from a howling wind (she was both the flame and the wind). A musician client visualised travelling to other realms to make music. An overwhelmed mother said that she felt like an animal running from predators in her mind.

I saw a middle-aged woman who said that she was drinking too much at night while her husband was away. Using the techniques in the session, she realised that part of her was stuck in an attic; she felt like a young child, remembering the feeling of waiting for her mother to collect her. Her mother had been abandoning and neglectful and, in response, this woman had created a lost child self in her mind. Her husband normally protected (fathered) this lost child but when he was away, the lost child surfaced with no parents. This led her to drink, in order to bury the resulting fear.

Another client had suffered a heart attack in his forties and could no longer work in a high-stress environment. He had been stuck in this trauma for several years and had been unable to move through it. In his mind, he was frozen in time and space. His relationships were crumbling around him. We had to 'melt his emotions' and shift his understanding of his purpose.

I had one session with a CEO who was working through some issues with his role in his company. As he was speaking, I developed four clear images based on the patterns of speech he used: a visionary, a wizard tinkering with technology, a fearful rabbit trying to escape and a crying child. I asked him if I could share the images I was seeing. He agreed and, after I told him, he thought for a moment.

'I can see that this process might involve a degree of vulnerability,' he said.

'Well, yes, of course,' I replied. 'Vulnerability and power are two sides of the same coin. If you want to step fully into your power, you need to embrace your core vulnerabilities. Otherwise you will always be running away from something, rather than expanding and moving towards something.'

'Hmmm,' he paused and considered what I had said.

I thought he was about to get up and leave when he spoke: 'Those images you gave me. They actually sum up my life.'

In a session, another client said that he wanted to transform the culture of his work environment. As I took a tour around his workplace, I could see why people were having problems in the office. I was struck by the lack of natural light and the large quantity of fluorescent lights. The windows were frosted and opaque, making the space artificially dark, with no connection to the outside world. The desks were divided into rows of cubicles and there was a *Mission and Values Statement* on the wall that had no resonance with the day-to-day running of the company. The business required staff to spend long periods consulting at client premises, so the employees were rarely, if ever, in the office.

They were looking for a quick fix to their 'culture' problem, but the company was following the laws of 'quick growth, unconscious capitalism'. This profit-making strategy was more important than the experience of their employees. I told my client that people become engaged in their work culture when they feel a sense of personal mastery in the workplace. To change the culture, I wanted to get a sense of the inner experience of all the employees. I needed to find the leaks in the collective consciousness of the workplace, then plug them. I started with one-on-one sessions with employees, to gauge their experience of the workplace. I then facilitated an 'open forum' meeting with all team members present and encouraged a no-holds-barred discussion, to create a culture of authenticity, openness and honesty.

This is how consciousness can be introduced to companies in a practical way. I start by reading the flow of consciousness: it is either blocked or flowing. If consciousness is flowing, things feel good. If it is blocked, we need to find the blockages and clear them.

In their sessions, clients talk about their family members, colleagues and life situations, and I create a picture of their consciousness, to establish what they are trying to process and move through by engaging in their experience. From my perspective, the stories they tell are all just simulated scripts that have been created to reveal their evolutionary lessons. The circumstances that we all consider to dictate our lives (family, colleagues, friends, business, economy, technology, investors, politics and hurdles) are always just mirrors of our internal state. Life is our own personal psychological drama, with the people around us merely representing the characters in our head.

Our 'problems' are not real from our mind's perspective—they are just props and mirrors on the stage, urging us to open up to our truth.

I start my sessions with clients by telling them that transformation only exists in one place: beyond our thoughts and stories. They can spend time in a hospital or a retreat, have a massage once a day, go on a holiday, start eating organic foods, fall in love, leave their partner or quit their job. But unless they learn to navigate their minds, they ultimately will not change. They will not feel any different. Unless we inhabit a higher perspective, we will remain stuck in our repetitive stories (our 'orbit'). So in each session I spend with a client, we put their stories to one side and activate their consciousness.

This is my training coming together: the academic in me analyses and identifies the issues; the lawyer in me uses all the evidence; and the philosopher in me links the issues to images, metaphors, mythologies and selves. Using all of these parts reminds me that there are no wasted experiences—everything we have done ultimately becomes a resource.

This is what I have discovered: our life is defined by the tiny choices we make in each moment about how to think, feel, sense and act. These tiny choices lay out a track in front of us that ultimately becomes our life path. Happiness, meaning, fulfilment and wholeness can only ever come from aligning with the being/awareness/consciousness that observes our life. We align with our consciousness by bringing awareness to our thoughts, feelings, sensations and actions.

So if we want to be happy, want meaning in our lives and want to feel whole, we must develop self-awareness. Conscious awareness helps us bring **all of our selves** into each moment, and it also allows us to clearly define and visualise our future. Being conscious and aware means that our lives are no longer controlled by our overthinking, repetitive, culturally conditioned, 'someone like me' brain.

The remainder of the book is a practical guide to getting conscious, using the four elements of awareness:

1: **Feel**   Honour all of your emotions.
2: **Think**   Choose only positive thoughts and learn how to direct your brain.
3: **Sense**   Trust your senses and the messages of your body.
4: **Act**   Work with the flow of life and love.

PART 2 · A GUIDE TO THE FOUR ELEMENTS OF CONSCIOUS AWARENESS

ELEMENT 1

FEEL

CHAPTER 11

Honour All of Your Emotions

☐ John dreams of being the nation's leader, and he has it in him to get there. He is charismatic, intelligent, visionary and hardworking. He's also a womaniser. Rachel, the journalist, is in love with him. What's not to love? On the surface, he's an eligible bachelor. But behind closed doors, he is a narcissist—an emotional parasite, taking what he needs from her and then discarding the remains.

In her working life, Rachel is forthright and perceptive. Her writing is witty and incisive. Her professional persona is empowered and she is very well connected. And then John calls. Her armour disintegrates with his number flashing on her phone. She is suddenly a small child, desperate for him to love her in the way she craves so deeply.

John knows that women seem to like him more when he keeps them guessing and that it isn't difficult to string someone along. For him, sex with women is just a physical outlet; but he is ashamed of the fact that he honestly could just have sex with any remotely attractive woman. He realises that he needs to have just one partner for a while; it is becoming embarrassing to be with so many women. And Rachel could be the girl. She is smart, attractive and well connected.

But John doesn't know how to fulfil Rachel's emotional needs—she is so needy! So he just ignores her until his desire takes over. If he ever has moments when he feels guilty about his relationship, he consoles himself with the good work he will eventually do for the homeless and the struggling workers. He is a good person. He just always feels as if he is running from something. And deep down, he is terrified that he will never find what he wants.

Rachel doesn't know why she holds on so tightly to the edge of a ship that is constantly trying to throw her off. In her honest moments, she knows she should leave John and find someone who actually loves her. But on the other hand, if she found that person, would she really want a diamond ring and a home in the suburbs? When her friends speak about buying houses with backyards and enrolling their children into schools, her insides churn and she feels like running. She has worked as a journalist in many places and travelled all over the world. She is a free spirit at heart and doesn't really need the daily comfort of a steady man.

However, John is starting to scare her. Every time they act out their fantasies with each other, the sex becomes increasingly violent. In the beginning she loved it and declared that every other previous sexual experience paled by comparison. But now she is just scared of the lengths she will go to impress him and the lengths he will go to destroy her. He only likes her when she ignores him or pretends to hate him. She is being eaten away.

Inside John's mind

John (the would-be politician) believes that if he wins the love of the public then his inner child will receive the love he longs for. This drives him. He is electrified by winning people over. He loves the thrill of seducing anyone: men, women, communities and nations. He loves the power. However, his political career will eventually be hampered by his need for love and adoration. He is entering politics for himself, for deeply unconscious reasons. The best leader is self-contained and is not desperate for the approval of others. The best thing that this man could do is dedicate himself to one loving, faithful relationship. That would force him to realise that he is lovable, just because of who he intrinsically is.

At a young age, John learnt that needing love was dangerous. His father was a philandering workaholic, and his mother was too preoccupied with the toxic remnants of her marriage to attend to John's sensitivity. As a child, he subconsciously decided he would win his parents' love by winning the love of others. If the whole world loved him, then his parents would have to love him as well. This meant that a loving relationship with just one person wasn't ever a high priority. He needed the world to love him.

He has the ability to move a nation. But until John learns the art of self-love, he will be using the public rather than serving them. If he remains unconscious of this journey, his political career will be marked by a meteoric rise, and then a scandalous downfall . . . just like all of his other relationships with love have been. He will make the world fall in love with him, but he won't be able to sustain it.

Let's imagine that John has an inner revolution and gets conscious . . .

One evening, John is at a charity gala ball. He is in the middle of bidding in an auction for a night in a luxury hotel. He thinks it will be the ideal way to seduce a woman: maybe Rachel, maybe someone else. Everyone is cheering as the bids go higher—$5,000! $5,500! $6,000! Then someone across the room shouts out, '$15,000!' John has a moment when he feels as though he has travelled out of his body and is looking down on the situation. His best friend leans in and says, 'Mate, don't do it. This is out of control. You'll regret it.'

The organiser of the fundraiser, a woman he may have had sex with once (he thinks) is standing next to him, cheering: 'Come on, John! Do it, go higher!' Then she whispers in his ear, 'I'll make the hotel room worth your money.'

John suddenly feels short of breath. The room is spinning. He must have had too much to drink. All of it—the shouting, the women, the champagne, and the ballroom—starts to move in slow motion. He shakes his head at his friends and gets up and walks out of the room. He loosens his bowtie as he leaves the room, in an attempt to get some air. He keeps walking until he reaches the street. The feeling doesn't leave when he gets outside. In fact it gets worse. He thinks he is having a heart attack. He hails a cab and asks to be taken to the nearest hospital.

An hour later, the results come back. A panic attack. That's all. It wasn't a heart attack, brain tumour or stroke. It was a panic attack. The doctors prescribe rest and time away from work and alcohol.

John is rattled. On the way home from hospital, he throws

his phone out the cab window—his phone with all his contacts and 36 missed calls. Once he arrives home, John packs a bag and makes a booking on his laptop for a flight home to see his parents. He hasn't seen them in six months and they are always calling him, wondering what he's doing.

The next afternoon John arrives in his hometown, hires a car and drives to the house he grew up in. He opens the front door without knocking and his mother shrieks when she sees him. She pulls him to her, crying and whispering, 'Oh Johnny, I've missed you so much.' His father goes to shake his hand but John pulls him in to hug him. When John steps back, he sees tears in his father's eyes.

John stays with his parents for a few weeks. For the first week, he is lost and restless. He walks aimlessly around the house. He feels like a child again. His parents try to talk to him about what is going on, but he can't give them much information beyond what he knows. He was fine, and then he wasn't. He had a panic attack one night and felt like he needed to get away. End of story.

Then one day it hits him. John wants to write. He has always wanted to write. He had hidden his desire for writing by being a voracious reader.

He pulls out his laptop and, after answering several emails about whether he is still alive, John pulls up a fresh page and starts to write. The words just come to him and he writes for hours. He only stops when he can no longer keep his eyes open. The next morning John wakes excitedly and starts writing, even as he drinks his morning coffee. He writes of an explorer, a man just like him, losing himself in alcohol and women because he had lost his lust for life.

John contacts an editor friend from a big publishing house. He sends through the first half of his book with his email. His friend calls him that night and says he wants to publish: 'When can you get the rest of it to me? One of our big authors has fallen through from the spring print run and we urgently need a replacement. Your book and your timing are perfect.' John replies that he can finish by the end of the week and his dream run of writing continues.

Once he sends through the final copy, he drives into town with his parents to celebrate and have lunch. John's hometown is quaint and small, surrounded by boutique farms and paddocks. John only lived there as a child, until he went to boarding school at the age of twelve.

John goes on to write seventeen classic novels that bring him great fame. He now divides his time between the city and his hometown. He has developed a new relationship with his parents that gives him fresh insight into his own patterns and behaviour. John embodies the archetype of the romantic who can seduce anyone. But he starts to understand that there is more to leadership than seduction. Leadership is what happens after the seduction. True leaders do not try to seduce. John is much better suited to a career in the arts, where he can romance people with his writing.

He is still passionate about public service and starts a literacy foundation for underprivileged children and adults. Over the coming years, John continues to have relationships with many fascinating women who he considers to be his companions. But he finds that his greatest, most faithful and honest relationship is with his art and his readers. This is where he feels most intimate and most uncensored.

John is eventually declared a National Treasure and the voice of his generation.

Inside Rachel's mind

On the surface, Rachel wants to be respected as a journalist. She wants to influence public opinion. And she wants John to love her.

As the third child in a family of four daughters, Rachel was always the keen watcher, the family observer. As a child, she would write stories and fastidiously kept a journal. Rachel's father was a diplomat. The family moved from country to country and she attended seven schools in thirteen years. Her family were world travellers. Their 'sense of home' came from each other. Rachel's parents were rarely around. They left the girls with nannies most of the time, as they attended to their diplomatic duties. They had keen appetites for the finer things in life and children did not belong in their glamorous world.

Rachel perceived her parents as works of art that she couldn't touch or access. They always had the perfect thing to say or to wear. Rachel's clearest memories of her parents are when they were dressed to go out. The four girls would line up at the door to say goodbye. Their mother couldn't kiss them (lest she ruined her lipstick) but they were allowed to kiss her cheek. And that's how she feels about John . . . he's a work of art that she can't access. He lets her kiss him.

Let's imagine that Rachel has an inner revolution and gets conscious . . .

One night at a charity ball, John walks out in the middle of an auction. Rachel watches him leave the room; he doesn't give her a second look. Typical, she thinks. At first, she expects him to come back. He's probably in the bathroom or seducing some woman in a dark corner. Then, after an hour and two ignored texts, Rachel realises that he has abandoned her, his date, at a table filled with his friends and associates. They all look at her apologetically, as though this is not the first time he has done this. His best friend valiantly offers to take her home. 'You know how he is . . .' he shrugs.

Rachel declines the offer and walks into the crowded street outside the hotel. She vows there and then to change her course. For the first time in months, she feels resolute and determined, full of adrenaline and purpose. She walks the thirteen blocks to her apartment with a spring in her high-heeled step. No more John. No more men like John. She deletes his number on her phone. Email address. Gone.

That night, her dreams are vivid. She is being tossed around the deep, dark ocean. On waking, she realises that she loves the ferocity of the waves and storms and is drawn to experiences that simulate the dangerous deep blue sea, like her relationship with John. She needs to reclaim the power that she has always given away to powerful men. She is the ocean. She is ferocious. She is fearless and rhythmical, all at once.

Rachel is living out the pattern of the femme fatale. The femme fatale seeks power over men. Yet the femme fatale doesn't ultimately seek love—she wants to conquer her inner masculine. Rachel needs to become empowered by the fact that she doesn't want a traditional life of marriage and children. In fact, this woman needs to acknowledge the power of choosing the free spirit's path.

The relationship she needs to understand is the one she has with her own inner masculine. She chose to be in a tumultuous relationship with this man, to shift the way she perceives the masculine and feminine. She is currently exploring the dark side of the masculine/feminine divide and, if she remains unconscious, she will be defined by it and it will eventually destroy her. But, if she brings consciousness to it, she will move through and appreciate it as powerful learning and re-emerge in her identity as a guardian of truth.

On Monday morning, Rachel's new awareness sparks a change in her external reality. Her boss gives her a new assignment: she is going to be a foreign correspondent in Istanbul. If she accepts, she must leave within the week. Rachel is overjoyed. She rents out her apartment, packs up her things and embarks on her new life.

Rachel goes on to work in some of the most harrowing sites of political turmoil in the world. She meets sheiks, drug lords, presidents and terrorists. She reports from the frontlines where the underworld meets international politics. She has relationships with many men, but never marries.

Rachel's fundamental relationship is with the truth. She eventually wins a Pulitzer Prize for journalism.

CHAPTER 12

The Emotional Operating System

☐ When I was a young girl, I loved swimming in the ocean, reading books, writing, learning new things, being with my family and friends, and looking after my little sisters.

As an adult, I love swimming in the ocean, reading books, writing, learning new things, being with my family and friends, and looking after my children.

My core emotional experience hasn't changed—I still feel excited in the same way and disappointed in the same way. I still feel uplifted in the same way and melancholy in the same way. It's just that my adult emotions have different background scenery, different characters and different stories attached to them. My point is: the way we experience every emotion and the feelings that we generate (love, happiness, sadness, joy, excitement, accomplishment, fun, jealousy, grief, rage, fear, surprise) stay the same throughout our lives.

Our thoughts change as we age—but our emotions stay the same. For example, the emotions of joy, anger and love will feel the same for you throughout your life. They will not look the same, but they will **feel** the same.

Let's say that joy for you as a child came from riding a rollercoaster at a theme park, while joy for you as an adult comes from dancing with friends at a party. These experiences look different, but they both feel the same to you, and are labelled as 'joy' in your mind. It's all about how our mind categorises our emotions.

So while it may feel like your childhood is a series of long, lost memories, this could not be further from the truth. **Our inner child is our emotional compass.** It shapes our total emotional experience and lives on in us through our day-to-day emotional life. Every emotion and mood that we experience in our adult life is entirely based on the feelings and emotions we generated in our first few years. Our emotional nature— including our self-worth, self-love and capacity to love others—is linked to our earliest experiences as children.

This is why the first element of practising conscious awareness is honouring our emotions, because they all come from our child self. The first step of getting conscious is releasing our emotions with non-judgment and tenderness. Rather than burying, hiding or suppressing our emotions, we need to respond to them as we would respond to a child with the same experience.

The types of emotions we generated as a child are encoded in our brain as emotional programs. These programs form our **emotional operating system.** Every new event in our lives triggers a particular emotional program and generates the same feeling we had at some point in our childhood. Even if we cannot consciously remember parts of our childhood, our memories are stored in our minds and develop into our emotional sense of 'normal.' I call this our **orbit**: the cycle of emotions that we typically experience.

Our emotional programs are linked to distinctive 'selves' within us, such as our child self, our inner critic, our warrior, our hero, our victim, our destructive teenager, our nourishing parent, our storyteller and our lover.

Have you seen the movie *Inside Out*? It was released by Disney/Pixar in 2015 and I cheered to myself when I watched it, as it presents the idea of inner selves in a simple and fun way. The movie tells the story of an eleven-year-old girl from the perspective of her inner selves, including Joy, Sadness, Anger, Fear and Disgust. As in this movie, each of our emotional programs is linked to a self within us. For example, the emotion of joy might trigger the lover and the magical child. The emotion of sadness might trigger the victim and the lost child. The emotion of embarrassment might trigger the destructive teenager and the inner critic.

Inner selves are independent sub-personalities in our consciousness that have a name, a face, a body, a voice, an age, a manner of speaking and a style of dressing. Carl Jung called these selves 'archetypes.' However, you will discover that an inner self is much more complex than an archetype. Our inner selves have desires, pleasures and fears. They determine our moods, life choices and behaviour. They create our behavioural patterns.

In any given moment, we have an inner self being expressed through our mood, emotions, thoughts, senses or actions. We are completely taken over by that self, and transported to a time and place that it inhabits. Through our emotional orbit, we could go back years into the past or be transported into the future. For example, we might wake up in the morning feeling overcome by our five-year-old anxious child self and feel out of control and vulnerable. Or we may be taken over at midday by the teenage self in us, threatening to leave our responsibilities behind. In the afternoon, we could be the cool head in a crisis, embodying our calm, adult decision-maker. In the evening, we may temporarily embody our wise elder. All of these parts of us remain with us no matter what age we are on the surface, and we constantly shapeshift into different selves.

In my work with clients, I have found that the best way to get to know our inner selves is to answer the following questions:

- [ ] Which selves surface at different points in your life (for example, during stress, celebration, hard work, relaxation or decision-making)?
- [ ] Which selves emerge at different times in your week (for example, on Monday mornings, Saturday afternoons or in the middle of the night)?
- [ ] Which self or selves come out when you are experiencing different emotions?
- [ ] How old are these selves? How do they dress? What are their plans and dreams? What motivates them? What scares them?

Once you have an idea of this self or selves, you can become clear on their role in your life. All of our selves exist to help us in some way, even our inner critic, saboteur, judge and inner teenager. In my case, my inner critic helps me do my best. My inner judge is a sign I am not taking enough care of myself. My inner teenager is the way that I know I have taken on too much and she comes out complaining. When we feel conflicted or off track, this is because our selves are not lined up and harmonious. We may have disowned selves that are disconnected from the others, or all of our selves may not be 'talking to each other.'

Life is a process of bringing all of our selves together and creating integration. We must be able to take off our masks, and to see all of the selves that exist below the surface.

CHAPTER 13

Your Child Self, Your Orbit

☐ Our child self is the childlike sub-personality within us that remains in our psyche even after we have become adults. The concept of the child self is based on the child archetype in the psychology of Carl Jung. Our child self can be magical or lost. If it is magical, it is free to transform into the nourishing parent. If it is lost, it develops into the destructive teenager.

What do people say about you as a young child? Were you always laughing? Thoughtful? Loving? Strong-willed? Inquisitive? This is an insight into your inner child, and the way that you experience your emotional reality. If, for example, you were a very well-behaved child who wanted to get everything right, then adult reality for you will initially feel like another assignment that you want to excel in. If you were a free spirit as a child, then you will want your adult reality to feel like the open road. Some inner children are nervous and shy, others are eager to please, others are star performers, others are sports enthusiasts, and others are cheeky comedians. Some children are intense from the beginning and some children are filled with innocent wonder. Our inner child may be a shy introvert, a tap-dancing performer or a nurturing carer.

The identity we developed as children becomes our default setting when it comes to making life choices. We constantly ask ourselves: *What does 'someone like me' do in this situation?* To determine the programs and beliefs that have been encoded into your emotional system, ask yourself questions like: *What was rewarded for me as a child? What was my dominant emotional experience? Did I mostly feel fearful, out of control, unable to rely on anybody, secure, loved or excited? Was I encouraged? How was I encouraged? Was I honoured? Were there regular highs and lows, or was life stable for me?*

You may recognise the orbit of your child self in any one of the following emotional programs:

☐ Overwhelmed   *This is all too hard. I don't know what I'm doing.*

☐ Anxious   *I'm so worried, my heart is racing. I feel on edge; what if . . . ?*

☐ Sad   *I just want to cry. I feel like my heart is breaking.*

☐ Inadequate   *There's too much to work through. What's the point? I'm never going to change.*

☐ Defensive   *This is the biggest waste of time.*

☐ Disparaging   *Some people might be into this rubbish, but not me. I've got better things to do.*

☐ Excited/Curious   *This feels new and different. I wonder where it will take me.*

☐ Hopeful   *I really feel good about this. I just know I'll be transformed by the experience.*

☐ Eager to please   *How can I become good at this?*

☐ Frightened   *I'm so out of my depth. What if I turn into a freak?*

☐ Dependent   *I can't do this unless someone helps me.*

☐ Playful   *This is boring. I just want to go outside for a swim.*

☐ Mischievous   *I feel like laughing aloud. I really don't take myself this seriously.*

Our child self-tunes into behaviour that gets attention from parents, siblings, teachers and the environment, then this habit of attention seeking becomes our default emotional orientation as adults. So if you were given attention and identified as a child for being rebellious and creative, you will seek out jobs, relationships and experiences that also emphasise these traits. If you were persistently told that you were aggressive and 'naughty,' then this program will be built into your personality as you mature. What made you worthy of adult attention when you were a child is what you believe to be your identity as an adult.

Let me give some examples of how our emotional programs work. One child was apprehensive about going to school each morning. At the time, he was told to 'just get over it.' His father said, 'I don't like going to work either. It's life—get used to it.' This boy's original emotional response to school was encoded in his mind as the way he experienced his day-to-day responsibilities. It now presents as sadness and a sense of dread on a Monday morning on his way to work. He doesn't love his job, but he feels that this is just 'normal adult life.'

Another man has memories of being excluded or overlooked in social situations during his childhood. He was overweight when he was growing up and left out of friendship groups at school. He was told by his mother to 'put on a brave face' and keep up the small talk. She said that if he would just fit in and be like everyone else, they would like him. This was stored in his mind as an emotional program. Now, when he is socialising as an adult he feels anxious and on edge. He tries to get along with everyone and just fit in. To compensate for his anxiety, he drinks a lot of alcohol to help him relax.

A forty-year-old woman presented with relationship problems. She always struggled to get the attention of her father. She consistently felt dismissed by him, as though she was unworthy of his time and effort. As an adult, she feels unsatisfied by her relationships with men, because she has an emotional program stored in her mind that replays each time she enters an intimate relationship. Part of her emotional program is a belief that her partner's time is more important than hers. She nags her current partner to give her more attention and to take her out more. Yet even when he does the things she asks, it is never enough because her emotional program is set up for disappointment in relationships with men.

Another girl in her early twenties was the youngest and most beautiful of three sisters. She was lavished with compliments and gifts from her parents. She saw life as a playground and did not experience any kind of adversity. As an adult, she is desired by many men who ask to take her out. She loves throwing parties and has many friends. Joy for life is a familiar emotional program for her.

CHAPTER 14

Your Childhood Roles, Your Emotional Territory

☐ We all take on roles within our family unit that stay with us throughout our adult life. These roles may appear to be obvious, such as the demanding eldest child, the cute and lovable baby of the family, the abandoned child, the smart one, the serious one, or the rebellious one. But below the surface of the family dynamic, things become more complex. We might be the family patient, who embodies and expresses the vulnerability of other members. Or we might play the role of the invincible, hyper-responsible one, who is not allowed to be vulnerable. We might play the creative genius, who is not permitted to do anything that may appear to be 'normal' or conservative to the family. These roles are created and reinforced in the way that we talk to each other. We say things like: *You're such a victim. Why are you always complaining?* or *You're on another planet; you never know what's going on!* or *You're so intense! Lighten up!*

The roles we assume become the **emotional territory** that we hold for our family. If our parents or carers are unwilling to acknowledge aspects of their own minds (for example their vulnerability, weakness, disowned dreams or extreme desires), then often we as children take up this territory on their behalf. Every new child that is born becomes the vessel for any residual territory that has not been claimed by existing members of the family.

We spend a lifetime crafting ourselves, based on these childhood patterns. As children, we find the masks that seem to fit our personality, then become adult versions of them. Examples include the hyper-responsible pleaser, the performer, the comedian, the rebel, the healer, the antagonist, the athlete, the artist or the peacemaker. In many ways, these masks are helpful. Our masks help us to navigate a complex world. It is useful to have a consistent identity, in order to have a stable life and ongoing interactions with others. However, our masks limit our ability to experience our whole selves. After years of embodying these roles, we start to believe that they define us. We think our masks are the totality of who we are. We are convinced that our identities are set in stone and that we cannot change the patterns that we have developed over the course of our lives.

Our childhood roles can be deceiving, because they are often exaggerated or extreme versions of our core selves. Many adults find it challenging to spend time with their family of origin, because we unconsciously return to our original childhood roles and feel constrained without knowing why. Our childhood roles can become a cage of expectations that we feel constrained by.

CHAPTER 15

Emotional Alchemy

☐ When we bring awareness to our child self, we are able to turn our fears and insecurities into imagination and curiosity. This is **emotional alchemy**. Here are some exercises to help you transform the emotional programs stored in your child self.

What's underneath?

To find the emotional program that is driving your current behaviour or mood, ask yourself: *What's underneath this emotion?* Then repeat the question, until you reach the child self in you that originally felt that way.

For example, if your current emotion is anger . . .

Ask yourself: *What's underneath this emotion?*
Answer: *I feel out of control.*
Ask again: *What's underneath this emotion?*
Answer: *I feel like I am going to let people down.*
Ask again: *What's underneath this emotion?*
Answer: *I feel like I need to please others, so they will love me.*

Ask again: *What's underneath this emotion?*
Answer: *I feel like I am not good enough as I am.*

As we move deeper through our mind into our child self, we uncover the original emotional programs that drive our adult behaviour. When we arrive at the original emotion, we can bring comfort to our child self with new beliefs such as: *I am enough as I am. I am worthy. I am lovable because of who I am.* This is emotional alchemy, turning our original anger (lead) into a wonderful affirmation of our own worthiness (gold).

Prepare for a reunion

You are preparing to meet yourself as a young child. You might like to prepare your home as if you are awaiting a visit from an honoured guest.

Readying yourself to welcome home your beautiful child self is an exciting process. In anticipation of this special event, clear your home of all unwanted clutter. Dispose of anything in your home with holes, rips or stains that cannot be mended or removed. You may want to have the carpets or furniture steam cleaned. All of your clothes, books and furniture carry emotional energy. Only hold onto possessions that trigger positive emotions for you.

There are other tasks that you need to complete in readiness for your child's arrival. When I am in the late stages of pregnancy, I always find myself 'getting my affairs in order.' This decluttering has a huge impact on my peace of mind. I give away, recycle or dispose of any clothes, books, toys or furniture we no longer need. I organise my tax and financial records. Like all new parents, I clear a new space for the baby to occupy. I think about what the baby might need and make sure I have everything ready, to make my job easier when the baby is born.

You are cleansing your mental, emotional and physical space, to prepare yourself for the changes that await you. This might include rearranging furniture or changing the art on the walls. You may want to decorate your space with flowers or candles—any addition that makes you feel uplifted by your space.

Welcome home rituals

Now that you have prepared your home and yourself, you are ready to embrace your inner child. These rituals are about acknowledgment and recognition.

Ritual: Childhood photos

Create or look through a photo album (in digital or book form) that is an ode to your inner child. Find the photos that make you feel good about yourself. These are the ones you look at and say, 'Yes, that's me as a child!' You may only find one or two photos of yourself as a child that you connect with. If so, stick these in the album.

How old are you in the photos that you recognise yourself in? Are you two, four, five? What qualities do you display in the photos you connect with? In my album, my inner child is a four-year-old who loves to swim, sing, read and play. There are two types of photos that connect me with my inner child: the ones where I am beaming with happiness, and the ones where I am looking intently towards the camera or towards someone else in the photo. These are the two qualities I associate with my inner child: beaming happiness and intense thought.

As you are preparing your childhood album, play some music that you used to love as a child.

Ritual: Go back there

Take yourself back to the time when you were a young child. Call your parents, siblings, relatives or any friends who knew you as a child and ask them if they remember what you were like. This may feel a little self-centred, but this early stage of childhood was! You are going back there. You are recovering yourself. Immersing yourself in your history allows you to move forward freely, rather than unconsciously stuck in that time through fears and addictions.

Ritual: Triggers

As a child, what did you dream of and what terrified you? Do these things still terrify you now? Can you think of any triggers that may be underneath those fears? Ask for anything that no longer serves you to be cleared from your mind and body.

Ritual: Handwriting

Get out your journal or some paper and a pen. Using your *dominant hand*, write down questions of your inner child. You are talking to a child, so ask direct and simple questions. Here are some examples:

What is your name?
How old are you?
What do you like to do?

How do you feel today?
How are you expressed in my life?
What are you scared of?
What do you do when you are scared?

With your **non-dominant hand**, write your answers to the questions. As you are writing in your non-dominant hand, your writing will look like it did when you were a child. As you write the questions and answers, you will be surprised by how easy it is to connect with your inner child, and how defined your childlike nature is. It may also bring up some emotions that you haven't experienced in a while, so be prepared for anything.

Once your inner child has a clear voice, choose a current issue in your life and ask your child for guidance. Use the non-dominant hand to write or draw the answer.

Ritual: Yoga poses

In gratitude for contacting your inner child, try some yoga poses. The child pose and the pigeon pose will be nourishing. Return to these poses whenever you need to.

Now that you have identified the emotional programs of your inner child, it is time to meet your **lost inner child.** This is the part of you that carries all of your fear, shame and vulnerability. The following chapter tells the story of a lost man and a desperate girl.

CHAPTER 16

The Lost Man and the Desperate Girl

☐ Robert was born to a heroin-addicted mother. He was in hospital with withdrawal symptoms for two months after he was born. He was removed from his mother's care when he was a baby, and taken into foster care. Then he was returned to his violent father as a toddler. His mother spent his childhood in and out of jail, so he never had much to do with her. He turned to drugs as a young teenager, because it was the only way he could numb his pain. Drugs numbed the hole in his heart where his mother should have been.

His drug addiction led him into a life of crime, because it was easier to steal and use drugs than it was to develop an entirely new identity. His friends were all criminals and he felt like he belonged in that world. He never saw himself as a 'normal' person who would have a job, a house and a family of his own. He was an outcast, and so he found a life to match what he believed about himself. Now, the only time he ever knows happiness is during a high. Whenever he isn't on drugs, he feels pathetic and that he doesn't deserve to be happy, or even alive. He is broken.

One day, Robert met fifteen-year-old Hannah on the street. She ran away from home, because her father had been sexually abusing her since she was twelve. Hannah has only ever been violated by the men in her life. She fell in love with Robert, because she felt he needed her. He didn't want to violate her; he loved her.

They started using ice together. Since then, her mind has become scrambled and she feels aggressive all the time. She is enraged and violent. She doesn't recognise herself in the mirror. She doesn't know if she will ever be happy.

The lost child grows up

Robert believes that he simply needs more money, so that he can buy pleasure in the form of a drug high. He thinks that he would be happy if he could maintain his ice habit with a steady stream of money. This is an understandable belief, as he was born into a heightened state of arousal. He has never left the fight or flight state, because his body knew from the womb that his mother was never equipped to take care of him. In fact, his mother sabotaged his capacity for love from the moment he was conceived. After that, life with an abusive father taught him to protect his vulnerability with violence. His familiarity with ups and downs inevitably guided him into a life of drugs. This is what his physical reality has offered him.

The only way that Robert knows how to support himself is through crime. His friends are all criminals and he is known to the police. He has never been to jail, but he is on a good behaviour bond and he is prohibited from taking drugs as part of his bond.

On the surface, Hannah simply seeks a permanent escape from the hell she is living in. She is in love with drugs, because they give her a sense of invincibility for the first time in her life. They make her feel lively and happy. When she is high, she can look people in the eye. She can live on the streets with no fear. Even her father doesn't haunt her. When she is off drugs, she feels insecure and traumatised. She sees her father around every corner. She fidgets and fiddles. She doesn't know if life would be worth living without drugs.

The truth behind the lost child

What this broken man deeply needs is unconditional love. He would give his life to be loved as he should have been loved as a child. He has the soldier and martyr archetypes. The soldier is loyal, brave and will follow orders to the death. The martyr will sacrifice life to defend a cause or belief. He is learning life lessons about resilience in the face of deep suffering. In a strange way, this man's behaviour is showing his undying loyalty to his mother. Though she destroyed him, he is affirming her by adopting her lifestyle. He is showing her unconditional love. If he could become conscious of his capacity for devotion and great love, he would be capable of transforming anyone.

Hannah has a nurturing mother archetype within her. She has the capacity to offer deep, maternal love and unconditional acceptance. This is why broken men are drawn to her. This is why her father sexually assaulted her—he sought solace in her mother archetype from his deep, unconscious wounds of rejection and abuse from his own parents. In her childhood, her greatest gift became her greatest wound. Hannah is on an assignment to learn the true nature of forgiveness. In order to learn forgiveness, she must first endure suffering that almost breaks her. Then she must heal to the point where she can show love to the people who caused her to suffer. If she could become conscious of her inner lessons, this damaged girl would come to have gratitude for her father's actions, because he taught her the transformative power of forgiveness.

Hannah deeply seeks sacred security and a beautiful family. Sacred security feels like the protection of an oak tree. It is deeply rooted and has abundant shade. In her occasional lucid moments, she sees magazine covers in newsagencies and on billboards that have glossy covers of beautiful houses and smiling families. She momentarily has an instinctive sense of longing for a life like that, but then it seems too hard, and she can't stop thinking about the ice. She wishes she wasn't so damaged.

Healing his lost child

Let's imagine Robert has an instant transformation and heals his lost, inner child . . .

One morning he wakes up. He is coming down from drugs and has slept in a drug house that has been taken over by a motorcycle gang. The gang leadership have asked him to join and he has a number of initiations to complete before becoming a full member. Hannah is waiting for him to meet her for a drug hit in the city. The plan is for him to bring her the drugs from the house he is staying in.

For the first time, he doesn't want to do it. The thought of collecting drugs to share with Hannah makes him sick. It's as though some part of him is looking down from above on his situation and he suddenly sees everything differently. He doesn't want to be a part of this world anymore. He wonders if he is still high, but this feels clearer than a drug high. He is questioning everything. He immediately gets up and leaves the house, vowing to never return.

He walks out onto the street and the bright sunlight shines into his eyes, causing him to squint and cover his face. All of a sudden he feels ill and violently vomits in the front garden of the house. He looks back at the house and feels as though he is farewelling his old life. Goodbye to drugs. Goodbye to gangs. Goodbye to crime, violence and desperation. He starts walking in the direction of the train station and then breaks into a run. He cannot get away from there fast enough.

He meets Hannah in the city and tells her that he has a new plan for them. She wants the drugs and starts crying, but she follows him anyway. They take a bus to the nearest hospital, where Robert informs the triage nurse that they are ice addicts and need assistance to come off their addiction. The nurse is sceptical but Robert is defiant, and she has never seen two drug addicts voluntarily present themselves at the hospital on a Monday morning. She makes a phone call to the Withdrawal Unit adjacent to the hospital, where there happens to be two rooms available. The nurse finds a ward assistant to escort them there.

Over the next seven days, Robert has horrific withdrawals. He has drug cravings and an increased appetite. He is angry and exhausted, but he can't sleep. His whole body aches and he feels anxious. Then he starts having flashbacks to his childhood. He sees his father in the hospital room coming towards him, punching him and kicking him. Robert screams and tries to push him away, but his mother is standing in the corner of the room laughing. He tries to tell himself that the withdrawals are causing hallucinations but these experiences are so real—surely he can't be imagining this? He feels so strongly that his parents are here in the room with him. Even though they are abusive, this is all he has ever wanted. Then their images fade and he starts crying desperately.

Through the withdrawals, Robert never loses his resolve to get through them. He is disgusted by drugs. He will never touch them again.

His reality starts to respond to his new level of consciousness. One of the doctors overseeing his treatment comes to talk to him and tells him about an organisation that helps people in Robert's position. It is on a country property, where they train young people who are 'newly clean' to work as farmhands.

Robert jumps at the opportunity and thrives on the farm. The animals, particularly the horses, give him the unconditional love that he has been seeking. He has a gift for working with animals and, after a few years of service to the farm, the organisation decides to award Robert a scholarship to study veterinary science. He is delighted; for the first time in his life he feels a sense of purpose. The animals have given him a place to channel his love. The people in the town where he works call him an animal whisperer. He is now worthy of asking for Hannah's hand in marriage.

Healing her lost child

Let's imagine Hannah has an instant transformation and heals her lost inner child . . .

One morning Hannah is waiting in the city for Robert. He is bringing her drugs. She is anxiously playing with her sleeve. She shivers in the breeze. She sees Robert emerge from the train station and there is something different about him: he is walking with confidence and purpose. She has never seen him look like that before. Maybe he's already high? Hannah's heart starts beating in anticipation.

He reaches her and announces that he has a new plan for them. He sounds so different: so clear and decisive. He tells her that there will be no more drugs for either of them. Hannah shakes her head and starts to cry. He takes her hand and says, 'Come with me. I'm going to fix us.'

Somewhere, deep within her, below the cravings, Hannah knows he is right. As if in a trance, she follows him to the bus stop. They wait without speaking. They get on the bus and get off near the hospital. They walk into the hospital together and Hannah stands behind Robert, as he talks to the nurse at the front desk.

A man takes them to a building next to the hospital; it is a normal-looking house and doesn't look like part of the hospital. Hannah is ushered into a room where she waits for what seems like an hour, but it's probably only five minutes. A woman with a kind face enters and asks her hundreds of questions, as she fills in the answers on her clipboard.

Over the next week, Hannah goes to hell and back. They tell her that it will be easier for her, because she is young and new to drugs, so her body will bounce back quickly. But it's her father who haunts her. The memories of his abuse follow her around. They have acupuncture, art therapy and group sessions to help the process. Hannah loves the acupuncture.

After seven days, Hannah starts to feel emotions that she hasn't felt in years. She feels . . . hopeful. She feels excited about the future. Robert looks different too. His face is no longer worn or tense. He tells her about a rural program he is going to try. She tells Robert that she has always wanted to study nursing. He says that she can come and live with him on the farm and study nursing at a college only half an hour away. She agrees and they move to the facility together.

Hannah works in the farm kitchen. Normally people only stay for a few months, but Robert and Hannah stay on. They become part of the staff. Hannah feels a sense of purpose for the first time in her life. She shows promise in her bridging course and eventually gets the news that she is admitted into the nursing program. She is over the moon. She has everything she needs.

Hannah will go on to help and heal young girls just like her. She will take in damaged girls who have been victims of abuse and bring them back to life. Over time, she will come to realise that her father was a necessary part of her story; he taught her that she could discover her greatest potential in her darkest hour. She becomes a mother, not only to four children of her own, but to thousands of abused women looking for healing. Robert is the love of her life. They live on a farm together for the rest of their days.

One day, Hannah walks past some photographs on the wall of their home. She sees a happy family looking back at her and realises that she has created the life of her dreams.

CHAPTER 17

The Source of All Our Fears

☐ The times you were most embarrassed, vulnerable or ashamed. The times your face felt like it was on fire. The times you cried in public. The times you felt raw, exposed and defenceless. Our lost inner child contains our most compelling fears and our deepest vulnerability. Our lost child is found in our fears, compulsions, anxieties, sadness and destructive habits. Our inner child is insecure and dependent on the opinions of others. It is terrified of being excluded and becomes highly anxious. It may withdraw from others into a dream world. The disowned and traumatised lost child becomes the destructive teenager self in the adult. The lost child uses anything it can find to feel comforted, and these comforts turn into the toxic patterns and addictions of the destructive teenager.

Our lost child is prone to unconscious attacks, which are experiences when our mind is hijacked by the fight or flight response. During an unconscious attack, we lose our capacity to reason and we are unable to comfort ourselves without resorting to a defence mechanism, such as regression, acting out or dissociation. In our mind, we go back in time to being abandoned and neglected.

Both our lost child and our destructive teenager believe that everything we need is out in the world—because that was their first experience. When we were born, our needs were all met by people outside of us. The lost child was originally formed because our emotional needs were not adequately met. We needed somewhere to store our pain, and this became our lost child. The destructive teenager acts out the toxic habits, anxieties and unconscious attacks of the lost child.

The lost child and the destructive teenager

LOST CHILD QUALITIES

fear, doubt, anxiety, dependency, withdrawal and unconsciousattacks

DESTRUCTIVE TEENAGER QUALITIES

acting out, complaining, addictions, toxic relationships, sabotage, rejection of responsibility, anti-social behaviour

To find your lost child, ask yourself:
- ☐ *How do I experience vulnerability?*
- ☐ *How do I respond when I feel ashamed?*
- ☐ *What behaviours emerge when I feel threatened, disappointed, excluded or embarrassed?*

To find your destructive teenager, ask yourself:
- ☐ *How do I act out when I am under pressure?*
- ☐ *How do I behave inappropriately or anti-socially?*
- ☐ *What behaviours emerge when I am stressed?*

Affirmations for the lost child and the destructive teenager:
- ☐ *I am a witness to my life.*

☐ *I am my own guardian.*
☐ *I am what I choose to become.*

Write these affirmations down and put them in a prominent place where you will see them every day (beside your bed, on your desk or on the fridge). Say them aloud to yourself every night. Affirmations only work if you believe them, so if these don't resonate for you, then create some that do.

POSES

child pose and pigeon pose (use these poses in moments of challenge or gratitude).

Looking for parents

Our lost child spends its life looking for people to play the role of our mum and dad. We search for friends and lovers who can replace the role of our original mother or father figures, to help our lost child establish the conditions that make him or her feel secure and 'at home.' This doesn't necessarily mean that we find parental figures that are exactly the same as our parents. It means that we look for the traits in others that we associate with our parents, and the methods they used to reinforce our identity.

If we have negative memories of our parents, then we often go out into the world looking for an idealised parental figure in a partner. We create a montage of the perfect parent from different images: our friends' parents, television and film characters, fairytales, magazine or advertising pictures and our imagination. We then look for someone who resembles this idealised image of a parent. In doing this, we believe that we are finding our inner child the best 'home.' However, this match of the vulnerable child/idealised parent ultimately blocks real intimacy with our eventual partner, because we need them to remain as an idealised image, rather than allowing them to unfold as a real and flawed person. We cannot permit them to be weak or vulnerable, as this will be too confronting for our inner child and destroy the image that we have created of our partner as the perfect parent for us.

This child/idealised parent dynamic also keeps us in the role of the weak, dependent child. Think of the stereotype: an insecure woman in her twenties who marries the financially-secure older man in his forties or fifties. She is looking for a father figure, to make her feel safe and 'spoil' her in a way her father never could. Or a man might marry an extremely nurturing, maternal woman, to receive the love and affection that he missed out on after his mother passed away when he was a child. I know a woman who had an addict/alcoholic for a mother. She is searching for the 'perfect woman' partner, to replace the mother she feels she missed out on.

In all the above cases, the relationships are the result of a search for an idealised parental image. Without bringing a new consciousness to these dynamics, the relationships will eventually become unsatisfying, because the roles are frozen in time and do not allow for growth and expansion.

Become your nourishing guardian

To live the life we have imagined for ourselves, our lost child must feel nurtured and safe. Otherwise, each time we visualise something new or reach an obstacle, the lost child will be scared and screaming, and the destructive teenager will give up or do more damage. To embrace a new reality, our inner child needs an internal witness: a protector and a loving guardian. We must become this loving guardian. This decision is life-changing.

Loving and parenting our lost child is about letting go of all the behaviours that we use to numb our emotions and keep our lost child buried: alcohol, drugs, cigarettes, sugar, toxic sex, gambling, overwork or compulsive behaviours. We all know our poison. The first step is disposing of any items that may prompt destructive behaviours.

This also includes people. Actively take some space from any people in your life who cause you to feel inadequate, sad or unworthy. You don't want to expose your lost child to them during a time that he or she will be feeling vulnerable. When you feel a craving towards any of these old habits or people, recognise the craving as you running from the pain you endured as a child.

As you 're-parent' your lost child, treat yourself as you would treat a young child. Practise being a good parent to yourself with early nights, wholesome activities, nourishing food, self-care, pampering, daily exercise, daily baths, occasional treats and lots of fun. The most important role of the nourishing parent is building the child's trust. Your inner child needs to know that he or she will be well cared for. Children thrive on reliability and routines.

Rita Pierson said: *Every child deserves a champion, an adult who insists that they become the best they can possibly be.* You are now the champion of your inner child. Your lost child has been found. Once the lost child is healed, the destructive teenager will be tamed.

CHAPTER $\boxed{18}$

The World is a Playground— Be the Magical Child

☐ The times you were most alive, joyful and spontaneous. The times your heart was racing with excitement. The times you were held and comforted. The times you triumphed. The times someone stretched open their arms for you to run into. The times you felt larger than life. The times someone cared for you, when you were sick. These are all stored in our magical child.

The magical child expresses our love of life. It holds the belief that anything is possible and contains our potential for wholeness. Our magical child is found in our dreams, our fun, our curiosities and our passions. Our magical child is content, silly and playful. Our magical child sings, laughs and dances. It builds friendships and sandcastles. It goes on rides and holidays and wakes up on Christmas morning. It buys new clothes. It plays jokes and giggles. It carries a childlike sense of optimism.

When the magical child within us is witnessed and celebrated, it becomes our gateway to a life of conscious creation. Our magical child teaches us to live in wonder and curiosity, nurturing confidence, possibilities and optimism. It holds our wildest dreams and is connected to our highest joy. The magical child believes that we are capable of realising our intentions. When we begin to nurture our magical child, we are able to imagine the limitless possibilities of life. We become excited and more spontaneous. We start to have fun and trust that anything is possible.

Our magical child comes out in moments of authenticity and deep relaxation. This kind of relaxation is not superficial; it does not come from a holiday or a massage, though these things may help to draw it out. It does not come from a bottle of wine, though we may go looking for it there. It comes from feeling a sense of home within. It comes from the things we like to do when we are unhurried, unpressured and uninhibited. It comes from our moments of innocence and contentment.

The magical child

MAGICAL CHILD QUALITIES

wonder, hope, optimism, excitement, curiosity, unwavering belief

To find your magical child, ask yourself:
- ☐ *When am I in my most pure state?*
- ☐ *How do I have innocent fun?*
- ☐ *What three things make life worth living?*

Affirmations for the magical child:
- ☐ *Everything is possible.*
- ☐ *I can do anything I imagine.*

☐ *I have faith.*

Write these affirmations down and put them in a prominent place where you will see them every day (beside your bed, on your desk or on the fridge). Say them aloud to yourself every night.

POSE
happy baby (use this pose to honour your magical child).

Exercises for reconnecting with your magical child

What did you do as a child that made hours pass like minutes? Herein lies the key to your earthly pursuits.
CARL JUNG, FOUNDER OF ANALYTICAL PSYCHOLOGY

Memory sparks

What did you happily do for hours as a child? Think of a beautiful childhood memory. Go back there. Feel the feelings. Absorb the sensations. Who was in the memory? How old were you? How did you feel? Do you still seek out that feeling? Chances are, these things haven't changed much. The key to our life purpose is uncovered in our earliest interests and passions. These passions are often evident in the genre of books or films we are drawn to.

Play date

Organise a time when you can take your magical child on a play date. It can only be you on the play date—no extras, not even your own children. This is an important time for you to connect with your innate potential. You can ask your child where he or she would like to go (using the non-dominant hand exercise from Chapter 15).

If you don't get any feedback, I would suggest any kind of activity that sparks ideas and inspiration (for example, building sandcastles at the beach, visiting an art gallery, cycling around a park, bushwalking or stand-up paddleboarding). It is great to do something in nature. This is not supposed to be a chore; the play date needs to be genuinely enjoyable for you. You are not babysitting—you are reconnecting with your sense of childlike fun. You might watch a movie that you loved as a child or a new children's movie that has just been released. You might go to waterslides or swim at the beach. There are no rules. Let fun be your guide. Make sure you spend at least two hours by yourself, and stick with the play date until you find yourself immersed in it.

Wild creativity

This exercise is about reconnecting with your creativity through any medium you like: drawing, painting, sculpting, colouring in, singing or playing music. Spend an hour or so just playing around with your creativity. Again, this is supposed to be fun, not forced. How did you express yourself creatively as a child? Did you play an instrument? Did you sketch? Did you dance? Use any colourful drawing tools you have (crayons, textas, pencils, highlighters or different coloured pens). You can take your inner child shopping for these—I love the craft section of the newsagent for stickers, coloured paper and pens. Draw a symbol of your inner child. Allow anything to come through.

Be open to the process. Don't judge whether the drawing looks good. Just let your inner child express him/herself.

Reflecting on our emotions

☐ Each emotion we have is triggered by an experience from our childhood.

☐ Our childhood emotions live on in us, as emotional programs that replay throughout our adult lives.

☐ Our child self creates our 'orbit' around particular emotions, and our childhood roles determine the emotional territory that we inhabit.

☐ Our positive emotions were all stored in our 'magical' inner child, while our negative emotions were all stored in our 'lost' inner child.

☐ Our lost child becomes a destructive inner teenager, while our magical child evolves into a nourishing inner parent.

☐ Getting conscious of our emotions is about finding then loving our lost inner child, and celebrating our magical child.

Now we can move on to the next element of conscious awareness: **choosing our thoughts.**

ELEMENT 2

THINK

CHAPTER 19

Choose positive thoughts and learn how to direct your brain

☐ While all of our emotions need to be accepted, honoured and released, our thoughts must be chosen with great care. We must train ourselves to only choose positive, constructive thoughts.

Our thoughts are just stories we tell ourselves. Repeat: **our thoughts are just stories we tell ourselves.**

Clear, positive thoughts are laser beams that trigger positive emotions and create momentum for more positive thoughts. On the other hand, unmonitored negative or neutral thoughts are grenades thrown haphazardly into our emotional territory. We have no idea where they will land or the damage they will do.

Our thoughts are like different stations on a radio, and we are constantly tuning in. Each station represents a different type of thought that either lifts us up or brings us down. Like the vast array of books and movies that are made, our thoughts can come from any genre: romance, documentary, horror, news, comedy or historical fiction. While our emotions are programmed in from childhood and only transform through love and attention, we do have the power to consciously choose our thoughts.

Every thought is a choice to listen to a voice in you.

- ☐ Thought: *I need to lose weight* (triggers the ashamed and lost child).
- ☐ Thought: *This guy is so boring* (triggers the judgmental and destructive teenager).
- ☐ Thought: *I need a holiday* (triggers the inner victim).
- ☐ Thought: *I wish my kids didn't wake up so early* (triggers the inner martyr).
- ☐ Thought: *Maybe I should go for a walk* (triggers the hyper-vigilant adult).
- ☐ Thought: *I need to go to the bank* (triggers hyper-responsible, caretaking adult).

Now let's consider some positive thoughts:

- ☐ Thought: ~~I need to lose weight.~~ *I love my body. I'm going to make something healthy and delicious for dinner tonight* (triggers the warrior).
- ☐ Thought: ~~This guy is so boring.~~ *This guy is taking time to talk to me. He is helping me become a better listener* (triggers gratitude and curiosity).
- ☐ Thought: ~~I need a holiday.~~ *I will book my next holiday next week, even if it's just a weekend away. Where could I go? Who could I visit?* (triggers the magical child)
- ☐ Thought: ~~I wish my kids didn't wake up so early.~~ *I am so grateful that my kids are healthy and have so much energy* (triggers gratitude and empowered choice).

☐ Thought: ~~Maybe I should go for a walk.~~ *I am going for a walk this afternoon in beautiful sunshine. I'll ask my neighbour to join me* (triggers optimism and connectedness).

☐ Thought: ~~I need to go to the bank.~~ *I will pass the bank on my walk* (triggers creativity and openness to the flow of life).

Choosing our thoughts is vital, because our brains can't discriminate between reality and imagination. Studies at the Center for Brain and Cognition at the University of California, San Diego (led by Ramachandran in 2007), showed that the same parts of the brain light up whether we are performing an action ourselves, watching someone else do it, or **vividly imagining ourselves doing it.** If something affects us, whether it is a powerful thought, an argument, a movie, a radio interview or a book, **our brains cannot tell whether we are living through an actual experience, daydreaming or reading about it.**

Here are some examples that demonstrate the power of our thoughts.

1. In 1990, Jim Carrey was a struggling comedian, living in LA and trying to find success. Every night, he would drive his car around and visualise being sought after in his field. He would imagine directors being interested in him and people he respected saying to him: *I like your work.* **He did this simply to make himself feel better.** One day, he wrote himself a cheque for ten million dollars and dated it 'Thanksgiving 1995.' In the receipt section he wrote, 'For acting services rendered.' He put the cheque in his wallet and

it slowly faded and deteriorated. Just before Thanksgiving 1995, he found out that he was going to make ten million for the film *Dumb & Dumber*.

Writing himself a cheque was a concrete way of bringing conscious awareness to his intention. This awareness sparked a series of events that caused his intention to materialise.

2. In 1979, Ellen Langer, Professor of Psychology at Harvard University, conducted a study on whether it is possible to reverse the ageing process. Sixteen subjects 75 years or older were given a range of ageing tests to measure posture, physical strength, manual dexterity, perception, cognition, intelligence, short-term memory, hearing, sight, taste and finger length. The subjects were then divided into two groups.

    In the experimental group, eight men spent a week in a residential retreat that recreated the social/physical environment of 1959. This included television shows, magazines, newspapers and movies from that year. The men wore clothes from 1959. They were told to converse as though it were 1959, discussing the events of that year in the present tense. They were asked to provide biographies and photos of themselves as they were in 1959. After one week in this virtual journey back in time, all eight participants showed marked improvement in their hearing, memory, dexterity, appetite and general wellbeing.

    In the control group, the remaining eight men were sent to the same retreat the following week, with the same activities. 'But their bios were to be written in the past tense, their photos were of their current selves, and once at the retreat they would reminisce about the past and thus largely keep their minds focused on the fact that it was not 1959.' (Langer, *Counter Clockwise*, 2009, p. 8).

At the conclusion of the study, all of the participants showed improvement in hearing and memory. They all gained a small amount of weight and their grip strength improved. However, 'the experimental group showed greater improvement on joint flexibility, finger length (their arthritis diminished and they were able to straighten their fingers more) and manual dexterity. On intelligence tests, 63 percent of the experimental group improved their scores, compared to only 44 percent of the control group. There were also improvements in height, weight, gait and posture. Finally, we asked people unaware of the study's purpose to compare photos taken of the participants at the end of the week with those submitted at the beginning of the study. These objective observers judged that all of the experimental participants looked noticeably younger at the end of the study' (Langer, *Counter Clockwise*, 2009, p. 10). This study was groundbreaking in its findings that our physical markers of age are influenced by our 'someone like me' mind.

3. In 1969, Australian psychologist Alan Richardson took a random sample of basketball players and divided them into three groups. Over the course of twenty days, one group practised free throws for twenty minutes per day. The second group spent twenty minutes per day visualising themselves making free throws, but did not practise them. If they 'missed' the free throw in their mind, they would 'practise' getting the next shot right. The third group did not practise or visualise the free throws. After twenty

days, the first group who had practised the free throws improved 24%. **The group who only visualised the free throws improved a comparable 23%.** The group that did neither did not improve at all (Richardson, 1969). Both the group practising free throws and the group visualising free throws were training their minds to improve, either through repetition or imagination.

Our thoughts are real forces that influence our reality. Whatever we tell ourselves on a regular basis, we start to believe. Whatever we believe, we act upon. Whatever we act upon creates momentum in a particular direction. Our direction becomes our life path.

If there is some area of your life that is not currently serving you, then the stories you are telling about that area need to shift. In the following chapter, consider the story of Nicholas, a brilliant man who told himself the wrong stories.

CHAPTER 20

The Brilliant Thinkaholic

☐ Nicholas is a highly intelligent man. He came first in his class at law school, and then became the youngest person ever promoted to be junior partner in a prestigious multinational law firm. He lives in a luxurious apartment in New York, and enjoys all of the trappings of great wealth in that buzzing city. Since he has started earning over a million dollars a year, he has become very brand conscious and materialistic. He has to have the best of everything. In some ways, he is the envy of his friends. But they don't really want to spend time with him anymore, because he is always working and he has changed from the person they used to know.

Nicholas misses the connection he used to have with his friends but feels he can't socialise with them, because money has become an awkward issue: the 'elephant in the room.' He has just split up with his long-term girlfriend. He's not concerned about it though—they were fighting all the time, so it's better that he can focus more on work now. He has started to drink a lot, in order to connect with the people around him. Last week, he had sex with a waitress in a restaurant bathroom, just because she threw herself at him.

He is surrounded by greed and manipulation; he always has to keep his guard up. He has everything he ever wanted and more, but he's not happy. Even with all he has, there's something missing. He feels it every day. It's eating him up.

Nicholas tells himself that he simply wants more. He wants to win. He believes that his happiness will be found in more money, more influence, more possessions and more physical pleasure. He wants to be the peak human specimen. He wants to be fit and tone his body. He wants people to desire him. He wants people to serve him and he wants everything he owns to be expensive. These are the stories that he tells himself. He has money, success, possessions and physical pleasure. His outer life is a mirror of his inner stories.

And yet he is empty, unhappy and unfulfilled. Although Nicholas' mind is brilliant, he doesn't realise that—even if he had billions of dollars, several houses and was the most attractive and powerful man in the world—he would keep experiencing the emotion of desire (wanting more). Nicholas doesn't know what lights him up, so he tries to live out images of happiness. He seeks out expensive hotels and restaurants, glamorous clothes and striking women. These are all images from movies and magazines that have been filed in his brain under 'success.'

Nicholas is a thinkaholic. According to Nicholas, his brain is a beautiful place of grand thoughts and worldly power. He loves his brain, because it has taken him to an ivory tower of human existence. His brain is his drug, because it gives him a high and a false sense of security. As he gets older and acquires more responsibility, he will always need more of what his brain offers him. He is chasing a beautiful, magnetic tail.

THE BRILLIANT THINKAHOLIC

As he blindly follows his need to impress, he will desire more in the outside world, but he will never have enough of what he is seeking.

Ironically, Nicholas thinks he is on track to achieve the peak of human existence, when he is actually headed for a dead end. If he continues along his current path, Nicholas will need more alcohol and drugs to numb the feelings of emptiness, as he will be unable to come to terms with the fact that his desires do not bring fulfilment. While Nicholas believes that he is seeking the best of what life has to offer, he is actually seeking a different life beyond his thoughts.

Nicholas is lost in the maze of his brilliant mind. He does not realise that the life he has created is simply a reflection of his fears. Every confrontation, every encounter and every defeat is simply another chance for him to fight his demons. Without consciousness, he will spend the rest of his life simply fighting his inner battles and, as a result, miss the true gifts that life has to offer: love, interconnectedness and peace.

Let's imagine that this brilliant man gets conscious and has an inner revolution . . .

Nicholas begins to see that his entire life is simply a response to the emotions and fears he created as a child. Nicholas' father mocked and criticised him throughout his childhood. He repeatedly called him 'pathetic, a fool, an idiot and a moron.' Most of the time, however, his father ignored him. When he did acknowledge him, he simply referred to him as 'son number two.' His father had impossibly high expectations of him, and Nicholas never felt that he was able to achieve them. When Nicholas first ventured out into the world, he lacked confidence. He was intelligent, but unsophisticated.

At high school, Nicholas was cold, cruel and aggressive. He used his intelligence as armour to hide his inadequacies and to gain power over others. He would insult other students. He made few friends and enemies of his teachers.

When he reached university, he was surrounded by the types of men he dreamt of becoming—the men his father would have been proud of. He spent a year watching and imitating them, then crafted his social identity in their image. He practised being charming, charismatic and interested in sport. Eventually he became one of them. Nicholas saw the world as his father, and he wanted to take control of it by seeking success, power and prestige. His father died ten years ago but Nicholas is still driven by the impulse to impress him. It is such a deep drive that he doesn't even recognise it. Buried deeply underneath Nicholas' image of a brilliant man is a wounded child craving love.

As Nicholas becomes aware of his emotions and thoughts, he starts to see beyond his childhood wounds. The true brilliance of Nicholas is buried underneath layers of inadequacy. He realises that deep down he is seeking integrity and a sense of service. He wants to be lit up by his work, rather than just make money. Nicholas is creative and he stifled this creativity in order to become the 'powerful' man his father wanted him to be. He has the capacity to use his substantial gifts for the good of others, rather than to wield power. To do this, he needs to transform his need to impress into a desire to serve.

He propels the process of awareness by talking with a professional about his childhood relationships (particularly his relationship with his father). He works through to the original abandonment that was the source of his unworthiness. He starts to meditate on a daily basis, and spends time alone in silence.

Then, he begins to experience life in a new way. His sense of emptiness and desperation dissipates. It is replaced with a renewed purpose. He has found and transformed the lost child into the magical child.

He begins to see everyone (his colleagues, clients and friends) as a reflection of his psyche that he must make peace with, and not as opponents to be defeated. He stops using others as vehicles for domination and power plays. He doesn't feel like simply striving and winning anymore, because life has ceased to be a game with winners and losers. He starts to value new things. Nicholas embodies the powerful warrior, who is powerful enough to surrender to the present moment. He devotes his mind to serving the highest good of himself and others, rather than simply serving his small ego.

In walking this new path of consciousness, Nicholas' energy shifts. Within months of living this new philosophy, Nicholas works with a client who eventually asks him to join his firm of venture capitalists. Nicholas' new job is to identify emerging talent in the health and technology sectors. He allocates seed funding towards new ideas for life-changing medicines. He loves his new role and, for the first time in his life, he actually feels that his work is connected to a higher purpose, rather than simply being a reflection of his intelligence and his capacity to make money. His long-term girlfriend returns to his life as he opens his heart. He reconnects with his old friends. Nicholas starts to long for children of his own.

One day, he wakes up and feels whole.

CHAPTER 21

Meet Your Storyteller

Tension is who you think you should be.
Relaxation is who you are.

CHINESE PROVERB

☐ All the stories we have told ourselves have led us to this point. Every detail about our relationships, our finances, our families, our work and our level of happiness is based on a story that we have believed and acted on. We need to become aware of the stories we play through our minds. Our stories become our nonstop internal dialogues and personal dramas. The things we tell ourselves and identify with from moment to moment are the running commentary of our lives. We all have stories that occupy our minds, like: *I can't be happy until I find the perfect partner*, or *I'm sick*, or *I want my business to perform better*, or *I'm so stressed*, or *I need more money*.

If you can't seem to find the love of your life, then you possibly believe one of the following stories:

☐ I am unlovable.
☐ There is no one out there for me.
☐ I always sabotage relationships.

- ☐ Once someone gets to know the real me, they will realise that I am not the one they want.
- ☐ I'm just like my mother/father, and they don't have great relationships either.
- ☐ I am waiting for the perfect person.

If you can't seem to bring more abundance into your experience, then you possibly believe one of the following stories:

- ☐ Having money is greedy.
- ☐ There is so much inequality that I would feel guilty if I had more than others.
- ☐ It is unethical to earn a lot of money.
- ☐ I will become superficial if I have abundance.
- ☐ I will lose my capacity for empathy if I make a lot of money.
- ☐ My relationships will change for the worse if I make too much money.
- ☐ I will make my family and friends uncomfortable if I make more money than them.

All of our thoughts and stories are crafted by a master storyteller in our mind. The storyteller has many faces. It can masquerade as a concerned friend, but then transform into a critic and saboteur. The storyteller offers both criticism (why we need to change) and a solution (how we can change). Yet even when we make the change, the storyteller finds something else to criticise. It tells us that we aren't good enough, capable enough, beautiful enough, young enough, experienced enough or qualified enough to do what we want to do. It tries to avoid any kind of vulnerability. This storyteller is our adapted self—the self we use to get love from others. This storyteller convinces us to change, so that the world will approve of us. It tells us that, if we change, others will want us around. We will be valued.

This storyteller persistently compares us with the achievements of others and denies our intrinsic talents. It convinces us that we offer nothing extraordinary to the world. It overanalyses the reasons why our ideas are impossible. It gives us all the reasons why we can't leave a life of security to take risks and pursue our dreams. Our storyteller convinces us to work our way up corporate ladders, take jobs or study courses that do not light us up. Our storyteller wants the world to dictate our life purpose, rather than consciously creating it. The storyteller clings on to the world's ideas of safety, success and security. The storyteller does not trust our plans, because it is unable to let go of the world's plans.

We become a thinkaholic when we listen to and live by these stories.

The storyteller evaluates our talents, gifts and skills in comparison to others. Rather than just being 'us,' we are constantly judged according to other people. For example, we might be 'much gentler than the other students at school,' 'just like our grandfather,' 'quite good at drawing,' 'as beautiful as a model,' 'okay at maths,' 'excellent at sports' or 'very committed.' All of these evaluations are judged on an imaginary scale in comparison to others. We are deemed to be wealthy, intelligent, talented or beautiful based on the wealth, intelligence, talent and beauty of others. These judgements can be made casually (by parents, friends, mentors and partners) or formally (by teachers, professors, bosses or colleagues). We are constantly given feedback about who we are in relation to other people. By the time we are adults, we have collected thousands of details about ourselves, based on a scale of other people. These details merge to form our idea of ourselves. This idea becomes our false, unconscious self.

Most people spend their entire lives believing this false idea.

When we are living from this false self, we try to compete with others because we are not sure of who we are or where we are going. We turn up for the race to knowledge, the race to wealth, the race to beauty, the race to power, the race to creativity, the race to influence or the race to goodness. Then we run as fast as we can. We run in the hope that we will find ourselves along the way. When we live from our false self, we enter into competitions with the false selves of others. We decide that our authentic self will be found on the other side of winning such competitions. But that doesn't happen. We simply find more of our false self. We enhance the parts of our lives we are trying to run from. And we become even more familiar with the person that others think we are. The false self exhibits the same traits as anyone who is lost: it is anxious, competitive, desperate and survival-oriented, with highly-aroused sensations. We cannot create a meaningful life from the false self, because we are living in reaction to others.

Our stories and actions do not transform through criticism, judgement or shaming. Consciousness is not 'figured out' or analysed. It feels into awareness and truth, rather than rational and logical thoughts. Thank your old stories for the things they have brought you. Thank them for the learning, the relationships, the experiences and the strengths. Then shed your old stories in favour of some new ones.

STORYTELLER QUALITIES
*self-doubt, self-denial, comparison, competition, judgement
of self and others, sabotage, overanalysis*

Think of some comparisons and competitions that are alive in your life at the moment. **Then write down a list of the people you compete with and the areas of your life you compete in.** These are the places where your false self is alive and kicking. These are the places that you scream to the world for acceptance and value, and you believe that the people you compete with are somehow taking this away from you.

Consciously let go of your false identity.

Think of some powerful labels that you have carried around as your identity since childhood. Do these labels strengthen or weaken you? If a label weakens you, perform a 'letting go' ritual: write the label down on a piece of paper, then tear it up into small pieces and throw it in the bin or on a fire. Consciously disconnect from this label.

Think of the people that you feel tied to, even though your relationship with those people may have ended. These are the people that you think about regularly and feel triggered by, despite the fact that they are no longer in your life. If a comparison or competition weakens you, imagine that person standing in front of you and say to them: *I'm ready to let you go now. I'm ready to embody my genius.*

CHAPTER 22

Find Your Inner Genius

☐ Underneath all the striving to be someone the world loves, there is a place of quiet knowing. It is our genius self and **it delivers the thoughts we need to create the reality we want.** Our genius is our direct line to consciousness, and it simply waits for us to listen to its voice. Our genius has its own internal guidance system. Our genius has its own exceptional, natural, creative interests and abilities.

The genius within us knows that our thoughts and beliefs are malleable and can be reprogrammed. The genius is able to rewrite our life script and shape our mind into any outcome we want. A genius takes the gifts of their inner world and expresses them in the outer world in a new and creative way. Being a genius is a choice.

The Genius

GENIUS QUALITIES

clarity, creativity, confidence, curiosity, vision, focus, positivity

To find your genius, ask yourself:

☐ *What lights me up?*
☐ *What sparks my sense of freedom and curiosity?*

Affirmations for the genius:

- ☐ *I know who I am and I know what I want.*
- ☐ *I gently let go of pressure and follow my truth.*
- ☐ *I am worthy of living my dream life.*
- ☐ *My vision is my reality.*
- ☐ *I am clear.*
- ☐ *I can vividly see my dream life unfolding.*

Write these affirmations down and put them in a prominent place where you will see them every day (beside your bed, on your desk or on the fridge). Say them aloud to yourself every night.

POSES

Upward dog and downward dog (use these poses each day to reinvigorate your mental energy and connect with your highest visions).

Tree pose and standing forward fold pose (use these poses to reconnect with who you are).

Reprogram our thoughts

This is my point: our brains cannot be trusted to provide us with the thoughts we need to create the lives we desire. But there is hope! We all have the ability to reprogram our thoughts. No matter how far we have been led astray by our storyteller, we are able to change direction and set a new course. Activating our genius self starts by changing the stories we tell ourselves, moment after moment and day after day.

The following chapter shows you how to **reprogram your thoughts**.

CHAPTER 23

Overcome the Thinkaholic, Reprogram your Thoughts

☐ There are four ways to overcome the thinkaholic and reprogram your thoughts:

1. Only choose thoughts that make you feel good.
2. Set clear intentions to direct your thoughts.
3. Write new stories into your thoughts.
4. Tell magical stories.

Only choose thoughts that make you feel good

The work of consciousness is constantly choosing positive thoughts and letting go of the others. The storyteller offers you thoughts that drain you and make you feel unworthy, while your inner genius offers thoughts of hope and optimism.

You need to unplug from any negative ideas you have about yourself. You need to replace your current thought streams with affirmations like: *I am worthy* instead of *I don't deserve this; I love and honour my body* instead of *I am fat and I need to go on a diet.* So much of our day-to-day mood is a response to the internal dialogues that we habitually practise.

Ask yourself the following questions to help you choose your thoughts:

☐ *Is there a positive perspective on this thought?*
☐ *What would I say to a child if they expressed this thought to me?*

The key is to become aware of the patterns, habits and manipulations in your thoughts. To do this, ask yourself: *Is there any evidence for this thought?*

Set clear intentions to direct your thoughts

In order to choose thoughts that take you in a positive direction, you need to know where you want to go. The genius in us knows exactly what we want. The genius can articulate and clearly visualise a dream becoming reality. This clarity of vision creates new neural pathways in the brain.

Become a master of your reality by setting clear intentions for how you would like your life to unfold today, tomorrow, next week and in the years to come. The role of the genius is to constantly refine the highest vision. The more specific, the better. Your highest vision is multi-dimensional and includes:

☐ the emotions and experiences you want to invite into your life;
☐ the physical outcomes you seek in your life;
☐ your values and beliefs; and
☐ the ripple effect you create in the world.

Write new stories into your thoughts

Choose one area of your life that you feel could be improved. For example: finances and abundance; love and relationships; assertiveness or self-care.

What are some of the stories that reflect your attitudes towards this life area? For example:

I'm a hard worker, but my family has always been up and down with money. We make it quite easily and then we find a way of losing it.

OR

No matter how hard I try, I just can't seem to find the right person for me.

If you believe this story, what will you continue to attract? For example:

I'll keep attracting the same experience with money as my family, rather than my own money story.

OR

I will also have ups and downs with money. I will work hard in order to offset these ups and downs.

Write down specific statements about how this life area could be, if you tell yourself new stories about it. For example:

I have a steady, comfortable income stream that allows me to be debt free, have a great lifestyle, own my home and have a yearly overseas holiday.

Create a future based on this new story. For example:

I have a job that I love and I earn $x per year. My partner and I live in a beautiful home that we own outright. We travel each year to . . .

Write down these affirmations and stick them in a prominent place where you will see them each day.

If you are content and fulfilled in any area of your life, then continue to tell yourself the same stories about that area. If you want to change any aspect of your life, get conscious about your stories, and start telling different ones.

Question yourself to help you become aware of your thoughts. For example:

If this thought comes true, will that bring me closer to where I want to be in my life?

If the answer to this question is 'yes' then welcome the thought. If 'no' then release the thought, visualising it floating out of your head and up into the sky, like a helium balloon.

Once our genius has formulated the vision that we want to create, we then adopt an attitude of acting as though our vision is already on its way into our life. We assume that the preparations are being made. Like an architect who has been commissioned to draw up plans for a new building, we are confident that our vision will be realised. We spend each day visualising the outcome and feeling the emotions of the vision becoming reality.

Tell Magical Stories

Our genius flourishes when we tell ourselves magical stories. Magical stories go beyond the limitations of the visible, transcending time and space. They allow us to enter our imagination to become more than we ever dreamed possible. In this place, we can be unlimited, unbounded and infinite. In our consciousness, all surfaces and appearances melt away, so we are as powerful, beautiful and abundant as we can imagine.

Remember, our brain doesn't know the difference between our imagination and reality. The genius is not restricted by other peoples' limitations. Use your consciousness to plant the seeds of a magical reality and use your stories to help them grow.

Here are some questions that spark unlimited thinking:

- ☐ *What would you do if money was not an issue?*
- ☐ *What would you do if you could not fail?*
- ☐ *What would you do if you could start again at any age?*

Tell your brain that this is your new reality. This is powerful mental technology.

CHAPTER 24

Julia's Muse

☐ Once we have contacted our inner genius, we can continue the flow of creativity by discovering our inner muse. Our muse is our source of inspiration.

This is a story about how Julia embraced her inner muse . . .

Julia went through school and, in her words, was 'academically average.' After she finished school, she went out into the world believing that she was of average intelligence. She spent three years getting average marks in a generalist university course and then worked for two years in a corporate job. She never felt inspired and started to feel increasingly depressed. The men she met were all noncommittal. She never felt like she was good enough for the people she dated.

After one particularly harrowing week, Julia knew she needed to change and contacted a psychologist. In her first few sessions, she recovered her sensitive and creative inner child who never felt good enough. She slowly learnt how to show love and be attentive to her original feelings of inadequacy and insecurity. For a few weeks, she simply concentrated on being aware of her inner child. She stopped replying to the texts and social media prompts of men who didn't make her feel good about herself. The more she gave love and attention to her inner child, the more she was able to let go of her inadequacies and simply follow her curiosities. If something made her feel excited and curious, she said 'yes'; if something made her feel sad or unworthy, she said 'no.'

She realised that, underneath her insecurities, there were many things she loved to do. In particular, she discovered a love of needlework and embroidery. This started off as a secret hobby. She was a bit embarrassed about it and didn't mention it to her friends, because she thought it sounded old and boring. Every weekend, she would spend a couple of hours creating small patterns and pictures. Her hobby turned into a passion. She would spend the week at work, then on weekends she would scour art and craft shops to find designs and patterns.

One day, she became frustrated that she couldn't find the right pattern for an idea she had. She decided to create the pattern herself, which worked perfectly. She enjoyed the whole process of making the pattern so much that she decided to make others. She started participating in needlework forums and eventually created a website to share the patterns she designed and to connect with other embroiderers.

After getting a huge following online, Julia saw a niche for a modern approach to embroidery. She had so many requests for her patterns and designs that she set up an online shop on her website to sell them. She started giving classes to children and adults who wanted to learn embroidery. After six months of selling the embroidery patterns, she was able to quit her job.

Julia had discovered her muse.

There are a few points to note about Julia:

☐ When Julia first presented for guidance, she could have been diagnosed with depression and medicated for the rest of her life.

☐ Julia **did not suffer from depression**—Julia was **feeling depressed,** because she was literally 'pressing down' on herself and her potential.

☐ Julia was only ready to awaken her muse and creativity after she made the decision to commit to her inner work and started to show love to her inner child.

☐ The first steps in awakening Julia's muse were to withdraw from the external judgements about who she was (her false self) and to develop her internal guidance system about who she wanted to be.

☐ Julia could not have attracted abundance from a belief in her average abilities. Once she trusted her free spirit, abundance flowed to her as a natural consequence.

CHAPTER 25

Be Your Own Muse

☐ Our inner muse has an intimate knowledge of what inspires us. It is the strategic creative force that fuels our inner genius.

There are three ways to access your inner muse. Your muse comes through in your style, your interests and the places you like to visit. It expresses itself in the things that spark your interest: the section of the bookshop you gravitate towards; the types of people you follow on social media; the podcasts you listen to; the TED talks you watch; and the way you choose to spend a free weekend by yourself.

Find clues to your muse in your triggers

Who do you click or clash with? Before we learn to consciously identify and embrace our inner muse, we need to look for it in others. The people that we are drawn to, inspired by, triggered by or feel jealous of are all reflections of the genius within us that we have not yet recognised and claimed. Every person or character that we 'click with' or 'clash with' is a sign of a self within us that has been sparked and activated (think of any role models, enemies, book/film characters, best friends, colleagues or loved ones).

Write down five people who inspire you. They represent 'selves' in you that are yet to be awakened. Creativity is curiosity.

Describe your style

How do you dress? How do you decorate your room? What art are you drawn to? What are your favourite books, films and type of music? What five places would you love to visit?

Think about the media and social media you consume: websites, apps, television/radio programs, films, books and other forms of art. Do you like the way these media make you feel? Bring awareness to this response and try to be discerning with your choices.

Who and what is your muse exposed to?

Joy is contagious. We need to spend our time with people that we want to mirror—people we want to be like and people that we want to feel like. The Framingham Heart Study investigated the spread of happiness over twenty years and found that those who are surrounded by happy people 'are more likely to become happy in the future' (2008).

Surrounding ourselves with happy people extends to the music we listen to, the movies we watch, the websites we visit, the social media we follow and the books we read. Humans are social animals and we identify ourselves through social connections. We need to be discerning with the people and experiences that we absorb. We also need to become someone that others would want to mirror.

Consider the people that you are regularly exposed to. Is there anyone that you are mirroring or absorbing in a way that makes you feel negative? Next time you are in the company of this person, consciously remind yourself: *What they are feeling is **their** experience; not **my** experience. I do not assist this person by feeling what they are feeling.* Rise above their experience, or try to transform it by constantly bringing the focus back to the positive.

Reflecting on our thoughts

- [ ] Every thought we have is a story we are telling ourselves.
- [ ] Most of our thoughts are crafted by the false, adapted self in us; the self that we originally created in order to get love from our parents and the world.
- [ ] We believe that this self keeps us alive, so we keep it alive.
- [ ] Overcoming the false self and awakening our inner genius is the transformation of a lifetime.
- [ ] Becoming self-aware and conscious of our thoughts is about embracing our inner genius and muse.

Now we can move on to the next element of conscious awareness: **trusting our bodily sensations.**

ELEMENT 3

SENSE

CHAPTER 26

Trust the Sensations and Messages of Your Body

☐ Our body is the canvas that our thoughts and emotions are written onto. Our bodily sensations communicate where our energy is flowing. They can give us superhuman strength or show us our triggers, weak spots and vulnerabilities. While we can put on a brave or polished face to the world, **we can't hide our thoughts and emotions from our bodies.**

Think of your body as a hidden storeroom of all your thoughts and emotions.

Our body is a record of every choice we have ever made, even the small ones. If someone has spent a lot of time with their mind dominated by their lost child/destructive teenager, they will have developed numbing habits and addictions that have harmed their body. If someone constantly listens to the false self/storyteller, they will be exhausted and lacking energy. When we tell ourselves negative stories all the time, we use up our energy stores and this presents as physical exhaustion.

Our body reflects where we invest our mental and emotional energy. To achieve anything, we must direct our energy towards what we want. Whenever we give our positive or negative attention to a person, activity or issue, we invest parts of ourselves in them. It is like making a deposit in an energy bank. We give our attention and energy as deposits, then get returns on our investment. If we make investments of negative attention and energy, we will have returns of more negative attention and energy.

Live in a positive state

When it comes to our bodies, we all know what we **should** do . . . eat nourishing wholefoods, exercise, go to bed early, rise with the sun, work efficiently, limit alcohol and other drugs, practice yoga, drink a lot of water, meditate every day, etc.

But instead, we often eat sugar, stay up late, sleep in, avoid exercise, drink alcohol, watch TV and procrastinate. Why?

In every moment, our body is either reflecting positive thoughts and emotions or negative thoughts and emotions. In a positive state, our body is moving towards health and vitality. In its negative state, our body is moving towards illness and depletion.

Do you:

- ☐ find it hard to sleep at night **or** wake up feeling refreshed?
- ☐ feel depleted **or** vibrant?
- ☐ find yourself needing to constantly rest on the couch **or** do you have the energy to say 'yes' to all opportunities that light you up?
- ☐ feel your age **or** much older?

The answers to these questions provide clues as to whether our body is in a positive or negative state.

Our body is in a positive state when our thoughts and emotions are positive. In this positive state, our body becomes a **warrior**.

Our warrior self has the discipline, perseverance and courage of a soldier. It provides the power and fuel for our actions. It gets us out of bed each morning. It shows up, gets its hands dirty and gets the work done. Our warrior self blocks our ego habits, attachments and distractions, like a martial artist. Our warrior confronts our deepest fears and walks courageously into our darkness. It works through our shadow and our unfelt emotions. It takes leaps of faith. It takes our fear and turns it into fuel. The power of our warrior is in unwavering focus and devotion. Our warrior teaches us to remain faithful to the vision, even when we are faced with obstacles, doubts and disbelief.

Our body is in a negative state when our thoughts and emotions are negative. In this negative state, our body becomes a **victim**.

Our victim self is injured and weak. It makes excuses. It dwells in regrets and low moods. It scrolls through social media and procrastinates. It explains why we can't do what we want. It avoids risks, cowering from the world and from challenges. It drinks alcohol and eats unhealthy food. It lives in the past or the future, and forgets the present moment. It watches a screen instead of exercising. If our body is weak, then our thoughts begin to spiral into negativity and we lose perspective.

- ☐ How do you react to challenges?
- ☐ Where does fear show up in your body?
- ☐ Is your energy channelled in the right direction?
- ☐ Are you empowering or numbing your body?

CHAPTER 27

The Family Man and the Doctor

☐ Raj always wanted a family of his own. He believed that having a house, a wife and three children was a sign of his success and value in the world. But now he's acquired all of these things, he feels a sense of emptiness. He loves his family, but he had thought that being a self-sufficient adult would feel different. He thought that he would have overcome all of his inadequacies by now. And he doesn't know how to change the way he feels.

There is always something that needs to be done, and his life is consumed by looking after the children or going to work. He works hard for an IT company, but he hates his job. About a year ago, he began to watch pornography on the internet every night after his wife went to sleep. In the last few months, he has begun to experience severe stomach pain every morning before work.

He went to see his doctor about the stomach pain. Dr. Song is a lovely, gentle woman in her mid-thirties. He relayed his symptoms and she examined his abdomen. She gave a few suggestions as to what it might be, but said she needed to wait for blood test results to be conclusive. After fifteen minutes, his time was up.

'We'll figure out the source of the pain soon,' she said. Raj wasn't so sure.

After Raj left, the doctor took a moment to reflect. She had spent the past fifteen years studying to become a doctor. Now that she had 'made it,' she wasn't sure it had been worth the long nights and wasted opportunities for fun and love. She still didn't know what she wanted from her life. All she remembered was that she had been a studious young girl and then suddenly she'd finished school. The next fifteen years had been a haze of books and classes. Her husband—a fellow doctor—is very conservative. She wonders if there is somebody else out there that she might have met, if she hadn't been studying so hard. He was just the guy that was always on her roster at the hospital. He was the only single man that she regularly came into contact with.

Dr. Song and her husband are trying to have a family, but she has been unable to fall pregnant for over a year. At first she didn't question it, but now she wonders whether she is even able to conceive. Deep down, she doesn't know if she wants to have children with him, or at all.

Dr. Song spends her days patching up people's pain, but she never feels that she gets to the real cause underneath their problems. There simply isn't time. She has everything she ever wanted—she is finally a doctor. But there is something missing. She feels a sense of desolation. After she leaves work, she goes shopping and buys beautiful, expensive clothes. This connects her with the exotic richness and creativity that is lacking in her life.

Life is a game

In his physical reality, the family man seeks an acute escape from his monotonous, boring life. He is waiting for his children to grow up, so that he can have some freedom and live his life to the fullest. He is strangled by duty.

Raj does not realise that, when his children are grown, he will still struggle to feel happy. He is seeing happiness through a limited lens—he thinks that happiness is a life of constant excitement and thrills. Even if Raj were an adventure traveller or a spy, he would still eventually be met with his feelings of inadequacy. Raj's inner turmoil of not being able to find pleasure is now manifesting itself as chronic stomach pain. The body always reacts to the state of our inner world.

Raj deeply seeks a sense of purpose, to connect him with the consciousness beyond his limited 'boring' ego. He needs to go beyond the day-to-day world of highs and lows, to access a steady channel of power and meaning. He is sublimating his desire for true masculine power into watching porn. This is a false, shadow masculinity. Rather than just working on IT design, he needs to throw open his mind and connect with the higher design of life.

Let's simulate a conscious revolution for Raj . . .

One night Raj sits down to drink a beer after his wife and children have gone to bed. Finally, the house is quiet. He takes a sip and feels relaxed for the first time all day. He picks up his phone and sees that he has received one voicemail message. It is from his doctor: *I'm happy to say that your tests came back all clear. So there's no problem. Give me a call if you have any questions. Have a good evening.*

Raj's places his phone next to him on the couch. He exhales deeply. His relaxation and relief move quickly into exhaustion and he puts down his beer and lays his head on the pillow. Within minutes he enters a deep sleep.

Raj dreams that his life is a computer game. He is a warrior and has to move through stages, before he can be declared victorious. He has to master different styles of fighting, from martial arts to fencing. He has to find a partner and create children. He has to find a house to live in. The game is unbelievably real and three-dimensional. The graphics are incredible and Raj is buzzing.

Raj rushes to his desk. He opens his computer and starts searching for the warrior game he has just experienced. There's no trace of it. He knows he needs to design it. He wants to write a computer program for boys and men just like him, who feel powerless and confused in their day-to-day lives. Raj feels excited for the first time in years. The thought of watching porn makes him feel sick, in comparison to this pure feeling of purpose.

He realises that he does love his wife and children. He had just lost his passion for life, in his quest for happiness.

Raj starts to play around with the control panel and the user interface for his game. He suddenly feels that his skills have relevance. He has been brought to life!

After many long weeks, Raj's first game is completed. He calls it Trans-Man. He sends his game to a contact in India who works at Robot Technologies. The company takes on his design and sells it to thousands of customers in India. His game is eventually acquired by Microsoft and distributed around the world. Within ten years, Raj becomes a well-known computer game designer.

By this time, Raj's children are grown and attending high school. His wife leaves him for his son's mathematics tutor. As they all move beyond his grasp, Raj catches himself yearning for the days when they were younger.

Suddenly, Raj wakes in a sweat. It is 3am. In a few short hours, this dream has taught Raj everything. He runs into his children's bedroom and kisses their peaceful faces. He runs into his bedroom and jumps on the bed, hugging his wife. She sits up, momentarily disoriented, and asks, 'What's going on? What's the matter?'

'I'm alive!' says Raj. 'The doctor called. I am not sick. And now I know exactly what I'm going to do!'

'What?' asks his wife.

'I'm going to write a computer game about a man, just like me.'

Emergency healing

In her surface reality, Dr. Song feels numb. She yearns for passion and vitality. She has 'made it' on the outside as a doctor, but she lost her spirit along the way. In the past few years since meeting her husband, she has never felt wild, free or unleashed. So she has begun to drink wine at night, before he gets home. He is very restrained and only drinks on special occasions. She keeps a bottle in the linen cupboard, behind the pillowslips. These days, it doesn't take her long to finish the bottle.

Her husband has become very controlling. He is a surgeon and he criticises her mercilessly, if she does anything he disapproves of. He doesn't like her friends. He doesn't like her to go out by herself when he is busy or working, because he believes that all of her spare time should be spent alone or with him. He records her menstrual cycle in his calendar. One night, a few weeks ago, he said that they must have sex because she was ovulating. Looking down, Dr. Song confessed that she wasn't sure if she wanted children just yet. Then he grabbed her wrist and led her to the bedroom saying, 'We agreed to have children. I didn't sign up for a barren wife!' Dr. Song cried as he thrust himself into her and silently prayed that she wouldn't get pregnant. The next morning, she stopped at a pharmacy and purchased a morning-after pill. There was no way she was taking any risks.

Dr. Song feels that she has replaced a controlling mother with a controlling husband. But recently her husband's narcissistic behaviour has made even her mother look nurturing and caring.

And now her work—the one thing that is hers alone—has become unfulfilling. After years of study and passing exams, Dr. Song feels limited by the constraints of general medicine. She cannot fix people in fifteen-minute sessions. Her dream of being a doctor has lost its shine. Now she would just like to have one true emotion. She feels out of touch with her body.

Let's simulate an inner revolution for Dr. Song . . .

One evening, her husband is away at a conference and Dr. Song has the house to herself. It feels so empty with just herself in it, after being told what to do by her husband for so long. Dr. Song wanders aimlessly around the house. After a couple of glasses of wine, she decides to turn on some music. She finds a track from when she was in high school and plays it on her phone. Before she knows it, she is dancing around the room. She is giddy and giggles occasionally, in spite of herself. She feels self-conscious, as though her husband is going to walk into the room and give her that scathing look—the one that comes before the inevitable question: *What on earth are you doing?*

She pushes the thought to the back of her mind and keeps dancing. At the end of the track she plays another, faster song. This is the feeling she has lost . . . the freedom and joy of movement. She remembers how much she loved dancing as a child. She had lessons when she was in primary school, but her mother put a stop to them when she turned twelve and needed to take studying seriously.

Dr. Song makes a snap decision to go online and find a local dance class. She locates one close to her home. It is a five-minute drive away and starts in half an hour. Dr. Song can't believe what she is doing. She runs into her room to change and sees her immaculate wardrobe of silk and cashmere. She starts tearing through it to find some gym clothes that should be there . . . In a drawer in the back she locates leggings and a T-shirt, then gets changed out of her serious suit into her dancing gear.

In the car, Dr. Song is alive with excitement and anticipation. Besides the secret stash of wine, this is the most outrageous thing she has done in years. She pays for the class at the door, but almost backs out when she sees men and women piling into the dance space. She doesn't get the chance to leave, as the teacher taps her on the shoulder on his way in. 'Are you coming or not?' he asks with a grin. 'I won't bite.'

It is a hip-hop class and Dr. Song feels ridiculous. She can't get the moves right and occasionally loses her footing. Yet she is having the time of her life! For once, she is doing something that hasn't been planned for weeks ahead. It isn't sensible or efficient. As her husband would say: *It's a complete waste of time.*

THE FAMILY MAN AND THE DOCTOR

On the way home, despite seven missed calls from her husband, she feels elated. She starts to remember the reasons she loved studying medicine so much. It was the thrill of the trauma room. The commotion of emergency. The life and death of it. The feeling of being part of something bigger than her.

She was originally an Emergency Resident Medical Officer but had transferred to general practice, because her husband had encouraged her to pursue a job that was 'good for mothers.' She realises that the sense of regret and desolation she currently feels is actually her detachment from her life path. Now she sits in a medical clinic talking to people about stomach pains and earaches, when she longs to be in a hospital working in the emergency department. That made her heart beat, just like the dancing had.

The truth is, Dr. Song doesn't want to have children. She was an only child and never felt loved by her parents. She never felt a sense of family. She was raised to be a machine and that is what she had become. A machine that fixes people. She is not mother material. And her husband isn't father material either. If they had a child together, they would just be repeating the patterns they had learnt as children.

The following day, Dr. Song applies to an emergency medicine recruitment agency. They contact her immediately and link her up with a prestigious hospital program in the city, where she can finish her residency program. 'Can you start next month?' the recruiter asks. Dr. Song feels giddy with joy. After she hangs up the phone, she gives the clinic where she works four weeks' notice of her resignation.

That night, Dr. Song starts packing her things. She is leaving her husband. He has been emotionally abusing her for many years and, since they were married, he has become increasingly controlling and possessive.

Dr. Song goes on to become a renowned trauma surgeon. She even visits war-torn regions, where she operates on wounded soldiers and civilians. She is finally free. She meets another surgeon who works for Doctors Without Borders and they fall in love. They live in different countries and only see one another every few months, but it is the kind of love that Dr. Song has been searching for all her life.

In taking a risk and freeing herself of her small reality, Dr. Song created the life of her dreams. She keeps dancing.

CHAPTER 28

Meet Your Victim

☐ When I was nineteen, I worked as a paralegal on my days off university. My job was to carry out property settlements. This job did not excite me in the slightest, but it paid well and it was a good job for a law student. During one particular semester, I had to work on Mondays from 9am to 4:30pm, and then attend university from 5pm to 9pm.

A twelve-hour day sounds like a walk in the park to me now, because I now love the work I do. But back then, I used to wake up every Monday morning feeling completely deprived of energy. I thought it was because I didn't get enough sleep, so I would try to go to bed early on Sunday nights. But even when I had over nine hours sleep, I would still wake up without the energy to get out of bed. I would calculate the hours until I would be back in bed again, then muster every inch of willpower to get myself out of bed. Even after I was up, I was plagued by a low mood. Everything felt like an effort: talking to people, walking to work. This was my victim self taking over my body. I had a constant sore throat. I lost weight. I was generally unhealthy. I would wait all week until I could go out on Saturday nights and drink, then lie on the couch and watch movies on Sundays. My relationship with my boyfriend at the time was volatile and

I was always distracted. These not-so-subtle messages from my body were signs that I was off track.

Here's the revelation: our victim self is not a sign that we are weak or lazy. Our victim is just the self that comes out to tell us that we are investing our physical energy in activities, jobs and people that are not part of our highest potential. Our pain and discomfort are simply our victim's way of communicating a blockage to us, like flashing lights on the dashboard telling us that the car needs more fuel, water or oil.

Far from being weak, the victim is one of our most robust selves. The victim is our reserve power system. When we have drained all of our willpower and strength but need to keep going, the victim appears. The victim takes energy directly from our body. We get sick. We are constantly run-down. We experience low moods. We have no energy for exercise or sex, let alone fun and creativity. The victim can wear pain as a badge of honour. It finds 'victim friends' when it connects with others on the basis of shared misery and common problems. In a victim mode, we all get together and complain how we are overworked, uninspired, unappreciated and demotivated. Although the victim treads water in the same place, it also prevents us from drowning. The victim can keep us treading water for years.

As the victim is built to conserve energy and get us back on the road as soon as possible, it uses a quick-fix approach. This approach treats the body as a machine, trying to escape and numb any pain or discomfort, rather than seeing it as a nudge or invitation. Consider these examples:

☐ *Can't sleep?*　　　　*Take a sleeping tablet.*
☐ *Feeling anxious?*　　*Have a drink.*

- ☐ *Feeling bored?*   *Eat some chocolate.*
- ☐ *Obsessive or sad thoughts?* *Take an antidepressant.*
- ☐ *Feeling out of control?*   *Cut out a food group and become food fixated.*

Anytime we feel distracted, overwhelmed, stressed or overshadowed, there's a tendency to escape, rather than going into the source of the pain and discovering its message. We maintain these patterns because we hope that escaping from our problems will help us overcome them. We believe that if we focus on our problems they will become inflated.

But it's the other way around. If we go into the pain, problem or discomfort, we can transform it.

The victim

Our victim emerges when our thoughts and emotions are out of alignment. The victim is actually a sign of strength and tenacity; it gets us through the day and keeps us from drowning. The victim doesn't know how to make positive or nourishing life choices. It only knows how to get us through the day.

VICTIM QUALITIES

making excuses, unreliable, low moods, extreme behaviours, distractible, complaining, regretful, cowering

Affirmations for the victim:
- ☐ *All parts of me hold the keys to my highest potential.*
- ☐ *My body reflects where I place my energy.*
- ☐ *I am healed.*

Write these affirmations down and put them in a prominent place where you will see them every day (beside your bed, on your desk or on the fridge). Say them aloud to yourself in the mirror.

POSES

Warrior one and reverse warrior (use these poses to activate yourpower).

CHAPTER 29

Heal Your Victim

☐ I recommend you use the following exercises to release blocked energy, negative emotions and heal your inner victim.

Identify the victim

Lie down and breathe deeply, then ask your body to communicate to you what it needs. What parts of your body are calling for your attention? Wait patiently until your body sends you a cue: an ache, a tingle or some kind of discomfort. (These cues indicate the places where you store pain in your body.)

What happens in your body when you have been overstretched or pushed too far? Do you cry? Get a cold? Feel a pain in your neck?

What behaviours emerge when you feel overworked, disempowered or victimised? Do you complain, act out, sabotage your relationships, overeat or drink?

Magnet visualisation

Use this exercise whenever you are feeling challenged, such as when you feel frustrated, angry, stressed, overwhelmed or anxious.

Find a comfortable position sitting, or lying down. Close your eyes and imagine a large magnet hovering over your body. Silently ask for any energy that doesn't belong to you to be released from your system. Visualise any unhelpful energy in a dark colour (grey or black) being pulled from your body and absorbed into the magnet.

You can use this exercise every day. It is particularly useful before bed, to release the energy that you have accumulated from other people throughout the day. This keeps you focused on your own path, rather than preoccupied with the energies of other people.

Lion's breath

This is another powerful tool to release any energy that is blocked in your system. You can use this at any time of the day to release negative emotions.

Deeply inhale through your mouth with your tongue in the shape of a straw. Then exhale through your mouth with 'lion's breath': open your mouth and stick out your tongue as far as you can, as you make a hissing noise. This is an effective release of emotions that no longer serve you.

From numbing to nourishment

As food is so closely linked to our emotions and energy levels, many of us reach for food when we really need to reach for a deep connection with ourselves.

Take a look at your existing patterns. Do you use food or alcohol to numb your emotions? This will lead to an unbalanced metabolism. Do you run on nervous energy and adrenaline? This pattern will lead to hormonal fluctuations and autoimmune problems. Is there a time of day, person or emotion that triggers you? We need to be as familiar with our victim self as we are with our surface self.

Step 1: Next time you feel triggered and crave unhealthy food, finish the following sentences in your mind: *Right now, I feel . . . . . . and I am using food to make me feel . . . . . . Instead, I can do . . . . . . to feel better.*

Step 2: Create a table like the one below and write a list of all the thoughts and behaviours you exhibit, when you are attempting to numb your feelings. Then make a list of the new thoughts and behaviours you can use to greet your deeper self with love, compassion and open arms, just as you would greet an unhappy loved one.

'Numbing' thoughts and behaviours	'Self-care' thoughts and behaviours
Thought: I feel scared and out of control.	*New Thought*: I am cared for and on track. I can control my responses to life.
Behaviour: Eating a tub of ice-cream.	*New Behaviour*: Having an aromatherapy bath.
Thought: I'm so tired and stressed. When is this going to end?	*New Thought*: My reality is in my hands. All I need to do is expand my energy and line up with my desired life.
Behaviour: Drinking a bottle of wine.	*New behaviour*: Going to a yoga class or for a walk with a family member or friend.

CHAPTER 30

Blocks in Your Body

☐ Underneath our victim is our 'shadow.' It is made up of all the emotions we choose to bury, and the parts of us that we rarely, if ever, enter. Our shadow contains our disowned, rejected, neglected, dark impulses, memories and characteristics. It is the combination of our lost child and destructive teenager, left alone to fester.

Experiencing our shadow

We experience our shadow in a variety of uncomfortable ways: it might feel like extreme self-loathing, or it might come out in the apathy of lying on the couch and saying, *I can't be bothered*. It might come out as screaming at your loved ones. We might stare at ourselves in the mirror and wonder how we might be enhanced: new hair colour, new lipstick, new clothes, a new face? We might eat and drink too much or use drugs to feel numb. We might become hypercritical and pick fights. We might have fantasies about the stranger or the ex. We might scour social media and other websites for hours. This is the self we hide from the world at all costs.

It's the habitual fights we have with our partner. It's our dark moods. It's the ongoing tensions at work. It's the destructive relationship. It's the weight we can't shift. It's the patterns we can never seem to overcome. Some people have a shadow that is characterised by complaining; they try hard to be positive and then fall back into the pattern of complaint. Some people have a shadow of depressive thoughts. Some people have a shadow of anger and they spend a lot of time dwelling on what someone did to them, or what they are going to do to someone else. Some people have constant headaches or chronic pain. Our shadow is our darkness, stored in our body.

Unfelt emotions

Our shadow is the accumulation of all the unfelt emotions we have stored away over our lifetime. Unfelt emotions are complex and painful feelings that we avoid and suppress, because they are too confronting to deal with at the time. They can arise from traumas, arguments, abuse, and any sadness or vulnerability that was unacknowledged.

We learn to 'unfeel' emotions from a very young age, perhaps before we can even remember. The seeds of our adult life are sown in the unfelt emotions of our childhood and adolescence. In fact, our adulthood is often lived in complete reaction to these wounds. We leave remnants of ourselves in our unfelt experiences and parts of us remain stuck there. So, someone with a lot of unfelt emotions can end up feeling like a shadow of their former self, because they have shed parts of themselves in every traumatic experience in their lives.

It's as if we have an attic door within our mind that stores all of our painful and traumatic emotions. Though we may hide from our unfelt emotions, we can't escape them—they are our constant feeling of heaviness or the dark cloud that follows us around. You may relate to the feeling of returning from a holiday and being weighed down by the routines and responsibilities of your life; that's how it feels to be reunited with our unfelt emotions. Our unfelt emotions get stored behind this locked door and they come together to form our shadow.

Our ball and chain

Our shadow is the part of us that resists change. It's our ball and chain. In analytical psychology, Carl Jung refers to the shadow as all of our repressed material that violates who we want to be and who we think we are. In Jung's words:

> . . . all the impulses, thoughts, wishes, and tendencies which run counter to the rational orientation of daily life are denied expression, thrust into the background, and finally fall into the unconscious. There all the things which we have repressed and suppressed, which we have deliberately ignored and devalued, gradually accumulate and, in time, acquire such force that they begin to influence consciousness. This influence would be in direct opposition to our conscious orientation . . .
>
> (Jung, 1964 [1918], para. 20–26)

The shadow consists of the material that we seek to repress or eradicate from who we are (Casement in Papadopoulos, 2006, p. 94). Therefore, the shadow relates to the material that we consistently attempt to eliminate or dissociate from ourselves.

Our darkness has been etched in our mind as our instinctual drives that must be suppressed, swallowed and denied. We are conditioned to avoid these impulses, and we judge ourselves when they lurk into our daily lives. There is a small group of people who are exposed to our dark side, generally limited to our partners, families, close friends and medical professionals.

If we do not face the shadow, our warrior spends all of its time keeping our shadow buried and ensuring that it does not rise. Occasionally the warrior is distracted or overwhelmed, and the darkness rises to the surface. The shadow is renewed by energy that matches its own: dark, buried and repressed. We sabotage ourselves so we can stay numb, instead of facing the pain that has built up. It's a strange spiral . . . when we are feeling down, we often act out in ways that are bound to bring about more unhappiness. With our shadow and our warrior in an ongoing dance, we leave our victim self to face the world.

If we would like to transform any aspect of our lives, our shadow needs conscious awareness and attention. Our shadow represents the combination of extremely powerful emotions. Ignoring or suppressing these drives keeps us away from our highest potential.

CHAPTER 31

Healing the Shadow Self— Susan's Eating Disorder

☐ In my practice with one-on-one clients, I convert the power of the shadow and self-sabotage into a healing process. We all seem to devote a lot of energy to sustaining sabotaging and self-destructive behaviours, so I take that energy and dedicate it to a new purpose. I worked intensively over eighteen months with a young woman who suffered from an eating disorder (I'll call her Susan).

Shadow Visualisation

During Susan's sessions, I facilitated visualisations where I took her out of her brain and into her consciousness. By accessing Susan's consciousness, we could directly contact the shadow self that was disowned and lost.

I began by guiding Susan into a relaxed and open state, and then I asked her to visualise the lost self or selves that we had discussed in our previous sessions. She told me that there was a part of her locked inside a brick house, and she described the brick house that she was stuck in:

There is no light in the house and everything is locked.
She is inside the house.
She looks like me but she is a dark shadow.
She is cold, naked and wet from the rain coming through the
*   holes in the roof.*
She is shivering in the corner.
And she hasn't been fed, so she is hungry and she is desperate.
Part of me feels motivated to help her, but part of me feels
*   angry at her too.*

This was Susan's self that was the source of her eating disorder. We discovered that this part of Susan had lived for a long time locked inside this brick house. This part had tried to make contact over the years, firstly through emotions like anxiety and panic, and then through toxic friendships. This was the disowned self's way of communicating to Susan: *See, the way this person makes you feel is the way I feel all the time!*

This part of Susan started throwing things and screaming from the brick house, to express her fear and desperation. This manifested itself as Susan's growing self-loathing. Eventually, because this part felt that Susan wasn't listening to her, her only choice was to create a situation so powerful and so destructive that Susan was forced to pay attention. Susan developed an eating disorder that led to hospitalisation.

Shadow Healing

I simulated the following healing for Susan to reclaim her shadow self:

You walk up to the house to save this lost part of you.

You come to the front door and you realise that the door is unlocked.

The padlocks that were on the door suddenly disappear.

You open the door and peer inside the house. It's pitch black so you can't see anything.

But as soon as you take a step inside the house, you are surrounded by white light.

And that lights up everything around you, as though your body is glowing.

You look around for this lost part of you and finally you see her in the corner.

She is curled up in a ball and she's crying. She is shivering. And you walk straight over to her.

Initially she is defensive and she moves away from you. She winces in retreat.

She doesn't know what you're going to do, and she doesn't trust you yet.

But you start talking to her.

You say: 'You can trust me. I'm here for you. I'm here to take you out of this place.'

And she says: 'How come you left me here for so long?'

You say: 'I was looking for you, but I couldn't find you. I lost you.'

She throws her arms around your neck and suddenly she is surrounded by the white light too.

She is transformed. She is no longer cold. She feels safe. She stops crying.

You pick her up and walk out the door. As you walk down the path away from the house,

you both turn around and you see that the house starts to crumble, brick by brick.

It continues to fall apart until the entire house is in pieces on the ground.

And that lost part of you is still in your arms, and you are both surrounded by light.

You find yourselves transported to a new and nurturing home.

You are both seated in front of a log fire in a warm room lit by candles.

You wrap her in a blanket and you say: 'Tell me everything that happened to you in the last sixteen years. Tell me when I lost you, how you survived and how it felt to be alone.

I'm sorry for leaving you. I'll never do it again.'

She says: 'I forgive you. We're together again now.'

And you both sit and stare at the fire for what seems like hours.

And then you turn to look back over at where she was sitting.

She is no longer there. She is now a part of you. She is inside you.

She has come to live in her new home in you.

And so you sit and look at the fire and you feel whole again.

And your body feels a new sense of vitality and love and wholeness.

You want to nourish yourself, because you feel complete. You want to move and celebrate

all the ways that your body can transform and perform.

And you want to celebrate life and people. And you want to develop your gifts.

Once we reclaimed and showed love towards this shadow (a lost inner child who had become a destructive teenager), Susan's food fixation became a lot less powerful and she was able to regulate her response to triggers. I am delighted to say that Susan was able to complete her final year of school and passed her exams. She was not readmitted to hospital for her eating disorder again. This is unusual for this type of illness, which often recurs for years.

The capacity for living a healed life is within all of us. Healing involves vividly imagining and embodying our healed life as much as possible, until it starts to resemble our reality. During my sessions with Susan, I said to her: 'For one hour every week when we spend time together, you do not have an eating disorder. You and I will both treat you as fully healed and thriving. Tell me what that feels like.'

Embodying her 'healed life' gave her a reference point for where her healing was taking her. She could see that she wasn't defined by or limited to her temporarily misdirected thought pathways. In taking this approach, we could access the power behind her 'dis-order' (there was extreme discipline and determination that we could reprogram from self-sabotage to self-love and healing). We used the power of her dis-order to create awareness. The key to her healing was in the form of self-love.

Another client was struggling in his marriage. His shadow self was showing up in his relationships. Using a similar approach I said to him: 'In our sessions, your relationship with your wife is fully healed. What does that feel like? What comes up for you if your relationship is healed?'

When we spend time imagining and embodying our healed lives, it is easy to spot the emotional programs and thought patterns that keep us unhealed. Before we can expect our bodies to be filled with energy, we must release our shadow material in a safe and healing way. The task is to transform our shadows into light. This new perspective invites the shadow to bubble up to the surface. In a safe space, we can notice the anxiety drumming away in our stomach. We uncover the ghosts that keep us from living out our wildest dreams. We then sit down and gently talk to that darkness, the anxiety and the ghosts until they are soothed. We treat our fears as we would treat a child who is afraid of the dark. And gradually, after committing ourselves to this unbridled self-love, we start to notice the dark becoming hazy and turning into a brilliant sunrise.

Love yourself enough to show up

It must be pointed out that healing requires dedication and commitment. Susan showed up to her sessions every single week, then twice a week for eighteen months when the work became tougher. She was committed to doing the work. Her desire to heal was stronger than her desire to stay in self-destruct mode. She was eager for the change.

I have had other clients who were on the precipice of change, who were ripe for transformation when, just at that point, they started to cancel their sessions. The cancellations were always at the last minute and for trivial reasons (for example, traffic or last minute study). I could tell that, even though there was a part of them that wanted to come, there was a stronger part that only knew how to sabotage their chances for healing.

Don't be ashamed—darkness is normal!

Whether working with a practitioner or on our own conscious path, a major part of transforming self-sabotage into self-love is normalising. We are all accustomed to burying our perceived weaknesses. As a result, we secretly tend to believe that our problems are embarrassing or shameful, that our darkness is darker than that of others, and that there is something weird or shocking about us that must remain hidden and cannot be exposed. Basically, we are convinced that we need to hide the parts of us that do not match our public mask.

If we want to grow and open up to others in an authentic way, we must shift these beliefs. We can shift these beliefs through the process of normalisation. Through this process, we name our 'darkness' as normal rather than pathological (caused by a physical or mental disease). Instead of thinking: *I'm weird and unlovable; I don't want anyone to see that* or *They won't like me if I am honest*, we must start to think: *I am a unique person with a lot to give. Sharing my vulnerability with people that I trust will create intimacy.*

We all have inadequacies, defences, insecurities, cravings, desires and impulses that we would not freely admit to others. We all have dark impulses that follow us around, until we heal them. There is no perfect person, relationship, family or workplace. There is no problem-free life for anyone. All of us have made wrong turns; but the people who thrive are the ones who do not drown in theirs. They put them into perspective. They are proactive about their problems. They channel their flaws into productive pursuits.

It's time to turn your tendency to self-sabotage into your greatest power. **Find your hero.**

CHAPTER 32

Find Your Hero—a Vision Quest

☐ This is your opportunity to do some excavation work to retrieve your shadow. Stage your own vision quest—go out into nature for a prolonged period. This might involve sitting in a park, on the beach or in your backyard for a few hours. You might go to a nature retreat, travel around the world for six months, or go away for a weekend, if these are options for you. Wherever you choose to go, make sure you are in a safe and supportive environment.

The retrieval process

During your vision quest, use the retrieval process to excavate your shadow. The retrieval process is particularly helpful for people who have experienced acute or prolonged trauma in their lives. One of the most courageous acts that a person can take is to go into their darkness. It's never going to be possible to relive every trauma that has ever happened to us. This is mainly because many of our traumas may have happened to us when we were children, too unaware of what was going on to even recall them. However, I believe that we have the capacity to retrieve the remnants of ourselves from significant trauma that is affecting our ability to live a functional and positive life.

The retrieval process can be undertaken during a vision quest in a natural environment. Once you have found a power spot alone in nature, here are the steps:

Step 1: Name a trauma or issue that still affects your life. This trauma could have happened last week, last year or twenty years ago.

Step 2: Allow yourself to relive the emotions that were felt during the trauma. Practise conscious breathing to stay calm during this process, or use the power of nature to make this process easier (eg. go for a swim in the ocean or sit at the base of an old tree to soak up its grounded energy). Allow the feelings to wash over you and try to experience them from a bird's-eye view. Observe the feelings hijacking your brain and body. Notice the powerful effect they have. And keep noticing the sensations until they lessen in their intensity.

If the feelings become too overwhelming or overpowering, then gently move out of the process and try again at a later time. In cases where the trauma is particularly harrowing, it may be helpful to be supported in the process by a psychiatrist, psychologist, coach, counsellor or psychotherapist. Depending on the intensity of the trauma, this retrieval process could unfold over a few hours or over a few years.

Step 3: Meditate in silence over the entanglement of emotions and wounds created at the time of the trauma. Think of all the people involved and how they were affected. Thank the emotions that you felt for getting you through those experiences at the time of the trauma. While they may have been unpleasant, these feelings sustained you at the time.

Step 4: Express forgiveness to everyone involved in the trauma, including yourself. In your mind, repeat the phrase: *I love you, I forgive you* to all of the people who were there.

Step 5: When you feel some sort of resolution and release, write in your journal to connect with your shadow (the parts of you that became disowned, in response to a lifetime of trauma). Ask your shadow questions about how it feels and how it is going to heal—it may feel that it has been wrongfully imprisoned for most of its life. Give your attention to your shadow. Sit with it. Do not try to 'fix' anything.

Step 6: Make a commitment to your shadow to stay connected. Create a ritual of checking in with your shadow each day, and give your shadow a new name. It is no longer your shadow; it has transformed into your greatest ally.

Step 7: Use sustained conscious attention to stay connected to your shadow and not fall back into old unconscious habits. This degree of consciousness will change your life and you will begin to feel truly free. You will realise that all of the threats and fears you perceived in the world were simply mirrors of your shadow. Once your fear of your shadow falls away, your fears in the outer world shrink as well.

CHAPTER 33

Call Your Warrior Home

☐ Once we have brought our shadow and our victim into the light, we can call the warrior into our body. Our warrior thrives when our thoughts and emotions are in complete alignment. Our warrior is freed when we release our shadow material. Until then, our warrior guards the door of our shadow, preventing it from sabotaging our lives.

When our inner warrior is activated and honoured, it rises to every challenge. It shows up to face the world every day and build the vision. It gives us sustained bursts of energy. Our warrior has stamina and determination. It knows how to protect us and support others. It can wear strong armour if required. It speaks our truth with passion. It uses mindfulness, movement and self-care with the discipline of a martial artist, to neutralise our black holes (regrets and shadows) and dark energies (lowest moods and vibrations). The warrior exercises, eats nutritious food, gets enough sleep and maintains optimal health.

Here are some indications that your warrior is empowered:

☐ You can rely on yourself to survive, physically, mentally and emotionally.
☐ You feel a powerful and intuitive connection with your body.

- [ ] You nourish and move your body well.
- [ ] You are able to defend and protect your honour.
- [ ] You feel connected to nature and to your extended tribe of family, friends and community.
- [ ] You are open to new experiences.
- [ ] You have the discipline to transform addictions and procrastination.
- [ ] You have the courage and capacity to follow through with your intentions, whether they involve simple objectives like exercising, or larger goals like starting the career you have always dreamed of.

Our power is ours alone. It is our unique way of getting things done. We all have this distinctive spirit. Yours may be enigmatic and resourceful. It may be strong-willed and decisive. It may be confident and assured. It may be passionate and determined. It may be loyal and disciplined. It may be quick thinking and flexible. It may be dogged and hardworking. We can only access our unique spirit if our warrior is focused and conscious in the present moment.

Channelling your power

How do you channel your power in the world? Often our warrior resembles the power that a particular animal uses to survive in the wild. It may pounce like a tiger. It may seduce like a cat. It may parade around like a peacock. It may keep its head down and work hard, like an ox or a workhorse. It may be strong and self-contained like a bear, until it becomes ferocious during a fight. This is your power animal—the one that most closely represents your warrior spirit.

We need to use our power to its full capacity. It helps to understand the way that our power works, and animals can be a useful reference point. How animals survive in the wild is a sign of how your warrior best survives. For example, if you identify with a dolphin, you will use intelligence, instincts, balance and harmony as your warrior powers; whereas if your warrior is more like a lion, you will use strength, courage and a mighty roar as your warrior powers.

The Warrior

Our warrior emerges when our thoughts and emotions are in alignment. A powerful body is the warrior's fuel.

WARRIOR QUALITIES
focus, determination, stamina, devotion, passion, courage, conviction, loyalty, reliability, honesty, trustworthiness

Affirmations for the warrior:
- ☐ *I keep to my word and honour my responsibilities.*
- ☐ *I show up and contribute every day.*
- ☐ *My power is reflected in my body.*

Write these affirmations down and put them in a prominent place where you will see them every day (beside your bed, on your desk or on the fridge). Say them aloud to yourself every night.

POSES
Warrior two and warrior three (use these poses to reinvigorate your body and connect with your highest visions).

CHAPTER 34

The Warrior Body

☐ The fuel of the warrior is the movement of the body. Think of famous warriors like William Wallace, Joan of Arc and Alexander the Great. They had to keep their bodies powerful, so that they could perform during battles. It is extremely difficult to activate the warrior if we are sleep-deprived, drained of energy and malnourished. Malnutrition can come from eating too little **and** from eating too much—in either case, the body is not receiving the right amount of nutrients to function well. A powerful body allows for a powerful warrior.

Conscious eating and exercise are an exciting phase of warrior consciousness, where we see our power being reflected in our body. As we begin to make more gentle and nourishing lifestyle choices, our bodies respond by feeling invigorated and strong. Our head clears. We feel robust. We have a surge of energy. People often say: *Listen to your body and to what it wants.* This is difficult advice to follow, because sometimes our bodies want red wine, chocolate and to sit on the couch for hours.

So the advice should actually be: ***Do whatever will maximise energy flow and lightness in your body.***

Develop a pattern of consciously tuning into your body, and asking: *What do I need to feel nourished and energised right now?*

Recognising progress

Focus on progress, not perfection—our bodies are not an achievement. Progress should feel like lightness, but don't become preoccupied with scales or calories. In fact, I would suggest avoiding scales and calories. You will know you have reached a conscious relationship with your body when you feel lighter (in body, brain and consciousness) and more powerful. You will get to the point where you want to honour your body, rather than punish it, control it or numb it. You will recognise progress in your feeling of vitality instead of dullness. You will glow and feel healthy. You will start to feel more energy and optimism. These are the desired outcomes.

Once we start to feel strong and healthy, our warrior will come alive.

This step of body power and awareness must be kept simple and positive: we need to remember that the body is just the base camp of the mountain. It is preparation for the climb, not the climb itself. Too many people get distracted by the body and do not see it for what it is: the first step of warrior consciousness. Some people become obsessed with the achievement of perfection and sexual appeal, rather than the maintenance of strength, vitality and resilience. This obsession leads to a fixation with things like weight, calories, food intake, nutritional values, diets, juices, supplements, sixpacks, breast sizes, clothes sizes, marathon times and gym classes. Beware . . . this is the false self in another form. The false self will tell us that we cannot grow or be happy until we have reached certain body goals. The false self insists that, once we are beautiful on the outside, we will have everything we want. The false self keeps us attached to our fears.

Nourishing and strengthening our bodies comes from an intuitive sense about what is healthy. We all have different body types and different body histories. We all know that it is good for us to eat whole, natural foods. We all know that our body feels alive and vital after vigorous movement, outdoor exercise and swimming. The body also craves communion with nature. Try to engage in body strength practices that can be sustained for the rest of your life.

A note about temporary lifestyle changes . . .

We all go through periods when we are sick, injured or working so hard that there is no time to exercise. I remember when I had my first baby and he didn't sleep through the night for ten to twelve months. I felt drained and tired all the time. Keeping awake through the day was a challenge, and the thought of exercising was the last thing on my mind. Prior to having a baby, I used to walk most days, play netball and practise yoga regularly. After a year of disruption from this weekly routine, I felt like I was in a bit of a rut.

In times like this, it is easy to fall into bad habits when even the thought of exercising again seems daunting. So be gentle with yourself. Do what you can, when you can. Get as much help as you can to get some fresh air in nature. If you can't go out, use a DVD or internet clip to do some exercise wherever you are. The body always responds to our intention: if we have a sustained intention to become healthy and nourished, our bodies will eventually mirror this.

Investments in our warrior power are:

- [ ] Sleep, rest and relaxation;
- [ ] Healthy eating and drinking water;
- [ ] Movement, fitness and team exercise; and
- [ ] Walking barefoot and swimming in nature.

These are time-honoured activities that will restore energy flow and lightness to our bodies.

CHAPTER 35

The Warrior Cleanse

☐ You may like to participate in a warrior cleanse for seven days straight. This has two effects:

1. Rids your body of toxins; and
2. Strengthens your warrior resolve and discipline.

For the warrior cleanse, you eliminate the following from your diet:

☐ Refined sugars
☐ Refined carbohydrates
☐ Caffeine
☐ Alcohol and other drugs, including cigarettes

You may consume the following:

☐ Fruit (in any quantity or form, ie. juiced or raw)
☐ Vegetables (in any quantity or form, particularly leafy green vegetables)
☐ Whole grains
☐ Organic, lean cuts of meat
☐ Nuts
☐ Water

Use this food table to create some new habits during your cleanse:

Current diet	When I eat this, I feel . . .	I will replace with . . .	When I eat this, I feel . . .
Eg. muffins as an afternoon snack	Bloated and full	A fruit salad, assorted nuts or raw bliss balls	Energised for longer—I avoid the afternoon slump
Eg. meat each night for dinner	Heavy and clogged	Vegetarian meals three times a week	Lighter and more regular
Eg. coffee three times a day	Wired and unable to relax	Two cups of peppermint tea daily	Well rested and calmer in the afternoons

What movement or exercise can you do this week to feel strong and powerful?

Current exercise	When I do this, I feel . . .	I will replace with . . .	When I do this, I feel . . .
Eg. I go for a 10km run once a week	Exhausted, with sore knees	A shorter run twice a week; team sports once a week	Less pain in my knees; I really look forward to the team sport
Eg. I don't exercise	Lazy, de-energised and sluggish	A brisk walk 3–4 times a week	I have more energy; feel great after exercise
Eg. I go to the gym five times a week	Tired and always hungry	2 gym classes and 2 yoga classes weekly	My appetite and energy levels have moderated; sleeping better

Reflecting on our sensations

☐ Our body is a reflection of our thoughts and emotions.

☐ When our thoughts and emotions are positive, we feel energised and healthy.

☐ When our thoughts and emotions are negative, we feel depleted and fatigued.

☐ We either embody the victim and shadow, or the warrior and hero.

☐ We can discover our hero through healing our shadow and undertaking a vision quest.

☐ We can invigorate our warrior body through a warrior cleanse.

Now we can move on to the next element of conscious awareness: **going with the flow of life.**

ELEMENT 4

ACT

CHAPTER 36

Go With the Flow of Life and Love

☐ A few years ago when sitting down to write, I would hope for inspiration. I would beg for the writing to flow: *Please don't make me force it . . .* In my mind, it was either going to happen or it wasn't.

One day I had an epiphany. Instead of hoping and begging for the writing to flow naturally, I began to ask: *What needs to be written through me today?*

Now, rather than seeing myself as a creator of the writing, I see myself as an instrument for it. My writing flows when it is coming through me, not from me. I simply have to show up and be a vessel for whatever needs to be written. This is not an abdication of responsibility. My responsibility is to be present at my desk, for a certain amount of time each day, prepared to write. I must work, but I must work with the flow.

Once I saw the wisdom of this in my writing, I started to see its application to my life in general. Rather than waking up and going out into the world with my sense of control about how I would like the world to be, I now ask: *What needs to come through me today?* By asking this question, I take the focus off my ideas about how I would like events to unfold, and I awaken myself to the collective intelligence of the planet. I listen to my inspiration and I follow the signs.

There is a flow of life and love, and all we need to do is go along with it. This flow travels through each moment, and we all have the power to line up with it. To go with the flow of life, ask yourself each day:

What needs to be expressed through me? ... and ... Who needs me to be a part of their purpose?

When we shift our perspective away from our nonstop ideas about how we think life **should** unfold, we are able to see ourselves as conscious participants in our collective experience. Our reality is an exquisite process of co-creation. **All other living beings are a part of this process.**

We can never know exactly how our vision will be realised. We can never know the people who will become our teachers, or how they will teach us. We can never know why we are in certain places at certain times, or why we make certain choices that lead us to our destiny. The chance opportunity, the synchronistic meeting and the irritating inconvenience can all be possibilities for the realisation of our visions.

The flow teaches us to surrender and to have gratitude for all of life.

We know when our actions are aligned with the flow of the moment, because they make us feel good and come from a place of love. Our brains are hardwired to feel good when we spread positivity around us. We get a rush when we smile at someone and they smile back; when we hold a door open for someone and they are grateful; when we have a soulful conversation with someone; or when we are doing work that makes a positive impact in the world. We feel good when we take the high road, choose silence or forgiveness, and include others.

Most of us are living on autopilot until we have everything we want (until we love ourselves). We believe that we must act on the outside before we can feel happy, inspired, grateful, abundant, trusting, spontaneous and joyful on the inside. We must have the perfect body or face; the high income and assets; the nourishing relationship and family; the great house and car; the right education and the holidays, before we can love and honour ourselves. We believe that it needs to show up on the outside before we can feel it on the inside.

But it's the other way round.

If we want to feel joy, happiness and love, we need to prioritise joy, happiness and love. We receive everything we want and need on the outside (the relationship, the body, the money, the house and the holidays), when we practise the art of self-love and align our thoughts and emotions. These are the keys to living the life we want. As Sarah-Jane discovered in the next story, they come first.

CHAPTER 37

The Beautiful Girl—All that Glitters

☐ Sarah-Jane is a beautiful girl who travels around the world as a model and DJ. Her dream is to be a famous actress. She is glamorous and attends all the right parties. She is used to being stared at. She is often given clothes by fashion brands and endorses a variety of beauty products. She regularly takes cocaine before DJ performances and catwalk shows. It began as an occasional high, but she now finds that she needs more cocaine in order to feel good. On the days after she takes it, when the parties are finally over, she stays alone in bed for hours in complete darkness and watches TV series. She spends a lot of her time on social media; her mood and her sense of self are dictated by how many 'likes' her photos get. Life used to feel like a wild ride, but recently it has started to feel like more of a blur.

Sarah-Jane is single, but she has had a series of relationships with much older men who are often married. She is terrified of ageing and recently had breast implants. She has had her nose done and regularly has botox and fillers. She spends much of her time exercising, having her hair coloured, getting spray tans, manicures and pedicures. She believes that she is only lovable and valuable because of her looks.

She wants to be in a relationship, but has a fear of settling down. She is scared of becoming like her old school friends. They all seem so boring with their normal jobs and kids. She has come too far to just go back to her hometown and settle down. Sometimes she wonders whether she keeps travelling because she is running from herself. She is on track to get everything she ever wanted and more, but she's not happy. Even with all this, there's something missing.

In the external world, Sarah-Jane desires fame and fortune. She genuinely believes that, once she is known worldwide, she will feel fulfilled. She also believes that her beauty is the key to her success, so she dedicates her time and effort towards maintaining her looks. Sarah-Jane's energy is invested in her appearance, and so this is where she invests her energy.

Yet even if Sarah-Jane performed to sellout crowds and had platinum albums and millions of dollars, she would still feel a hole inside. This is because they are external outcomes and she is seeking them to fill her up emotionally. At present, she is performing to reinforce her self-worth, rather than to channel joy. This is why she has started to rely on drugs to simulate the experience of happiness. She is disconnected from herself.

While this beautiful girl only feels valuable because of her external features, she will not achieve the outcomes she seeks. She can only connect with others in a limited capacity from her external mask. She has lost her way, because she believes that happiness exists outside of her—in the crowds and the money. She has no idea that the wholeness and value she seeks is contained within her. Even though she is a captivating performer, she will not feel 'happy' until she connects with her conscious nature.

Let's simulate an inner revolution for Sarah-Jane . . .

One day she wakes up. She is lying in a hotel room next to a married man she'd slept with after last night's party. She feels sick. She creeps out of bed and quietly gets dressed. She grabs her shoes and bag and leaves the room. As she makes her way barefoot down the hotel hallway to the elevator, she bursts into tears.

She decides in that moment to leave anything behind that interferes with her clarity and optimal functioning. To start with, Sarah-Jane vows to give up cocaine and to replace her habit of watching TV in the dark with a daily practice of yoga, journaling and meditation. She gets a taxi back to her apartment and showers. She goes straight to a yoga class.

Through her practice of journaling, Sarah-Jane reconnects with the emotional programs and attachments she developed as a child. From a young age, Sarah-Jane was highly valued because of her beauty. Her face and her body were her currency. She was constantly told how beautiful she was and received male attention wherever she went.

Her parents had an unstable marriage. Her father was an emotionally absent, high-flying entrepreneur; her mother was an ex-model who struggled to gain his respect. Her father frequently went on business trips and had late nights out, where he indulged in drugs and sex with prostitutes. He also had several affairs throughout the marriage, but her mother could never leave, because she didn't have the confidence to support herself. Her mother was also accustomed to her lavish lifestyle, and became increasingly dependent on alcohol to numb her pain.

Sarah-Jane was an only child, and was constantly torn between her parents. She was 'daddy's little girl' and he called her the most beautiful girl in the world. She was also her mother's confidante but felt powerless to help her. She became used to being the girl in the middle of their marriage. This is why she frequently has relationships with older, married men, in an attempt to make sense of her parents' marriage.

In her teen years, Sarah-Jane developed an eating disorder because, even though she was beautiful on the outside, she didn't love her body or herself. There was a disconnection between the external praise she received and her internal sense of self. At the time, she believed that if she changed her body, then she would begin to love herself. Eventually, an obsession with food was replaced by an obsession with fame. She became convinced that fame would bring her happiness, just as she was convinced that her perfect body weight would bring her happiness.

In her inner revolution, Sarah-Jane starts to switch off from fame and fortune as destinations that will make her feel whole. She sees that a pattern of 'ideal futurising' has become entrenched in her mind; that her happiness is always somewhere else—in another person, place or event in the future. Sarah-Jane realises that she can still pursue her work, but a sense of awareness and wholeness. With a lifestyle based on self-care, this beautiful girl begins to see that she can embody love and light for the world. Rather than abusing her body, she starts nurturing it with baths, fresh wholefoods and regular massages. She buys a bike and rides down to the beach near her home to swim in the mornings.

Sarah-Jane continues her daily meditation and yoga practice. She also chooses to read books again, rather than watch screens all the time. In her reading, she discovers the mythology of the goddess Aphrodite, who channels beauty, love and sexuality. She becomes fascinated by goddess mythology and devours information about it. She begins to study yoga teaching and, along with some friends, pioneers a new 'goddess yoga' studio, with Sarah-Jane as a DJ and teacher. She writes music for yoga, which brings light and celebration to the movement.

Sarah-Jane shifts her intentions, so that she no longer seeks fame as an end in itself. Rather, she wants to show the world that there is beauty, healing and joy in sound and movement. She is here to teach that we should endeavour to dance, sing and channel joy every day.

Connecting with her higher purpose brings meaning to her life. Once she does this, she can embody the highest forms of bliss. In her highest potential, Sarah-Jane is the embodiment of the lover. Her performances evolve and she touches millions with her unique combination of goddess yoga and music.

CHAPTER 38

Your Lover—Everything You Dream Of

☐ Our inner lover is the home of unconditional love, abundance, pleasure, ecstasy and unbridled joy. Our lover allows us to have a deep appreciation for basic life experiences. Our lover invites us to see wonder in the ordinary and beauty in simplicity. It is the haven that we retreat to in joy and solitude, in strength and self-care. It is a radiant sunset, a refreshing ocean swim, resonant music and rapturous dancing. Once we are able to surrender to the extraordinary love and tenderness that we feel for ourselves, we can open ourselves to the love of others and interconnectedness with other conscious beings.

Only someone who is united with their inner lover is able to truly love another person. When our inner lover feels genuinely honoured, it responds with unconditional love and gratitude. It cares for us and for others. It opens our arms. It relaxes and breathes. It knows that the present moment is all we ever have. It surrenders to the unknown forces beyond our control.

Our lover is also able to celebrate the realisation of past visions and prepare fertile ground for new visions to be imagined and born. In the unseen realm, we go with the flow of the universe and surrender to what each moment asks of us.

☐ When we act from our inner lover, we **go with the flow of life**. When we act from our inner saboteur, we try to control the outcome and block the flow.

☐ Our lover **lets life unfold before us**. Our saboteur struggles and pushes to get what we want.

☐ Our lover has a **deep passion for our work** and attracts abundance, to support the life we lead. Our saboteur finds the highest paying job, so that we can buy nice things and 'keep up' with our friends.

☐ Our lover **honours our relationships**, because we can't imagine spending our life with anyone else. Our saboteur criticises our partner, family and friends because they are 'not good enough.'

☐ Our lover has **everyday gratitude** for our life. Our saboteur always finds something wrong with it.

Choose the lover.

The lover

The lover uses self-love and self-care to overcome self-sabotage.

LOVER QUALITIES

gratitude, generosity, gentleness, peace, surrender, flow, alignment, acceptance

Affirmations for the lover:

☐ *Everyone I encounter is a teacher.*
☐ *We all have a place.*
☐ *I am grateful to all of life.*

Write these affirmations down and put them in a prominent place where you will see them every day (beside your bed, on your desk or on the fridge). Say these aloud to yourself in the mirror each night.

POSES

Mountain pose and garland pose (use these poses to express gratitude for your life).

Your dream life starts now

Today is the beginning of doing everything you have promised yourself you would do. Try these exercises to move towards a love-filled life.

1. **Make a list** of the things you intend to do, when you have everything in your life 'sorted,' for example:

   When I find a relationship, I will . . . . . . eg. stop drinking as much

   When I get promoted at work, I will . . . . . . eg. start to spend time with my family

   When I start earning a lot of money, I will . . . . . . eg. visit that place I always wanted to see

   When I believe that I'm beautiful, I will . . . . . . eg. relax and become more social and open with others

   Take a step towards one of these outcomes today.

2. **Choose one ongoing challenge** in your life that you can't understand or resolve. Ask yourself: *How would I feel if this issue was fully healed and resolved? What kind of person would*

I be? How would my life look? What is my vision for healing this conflict?

3. **Practise self-care.** Our inner lover needs our affection and attention. This exercise is about self-care and luxury. To connect with your inner lover, organise an indulgent and healing treatment: a massage, aromatherapy bath, facial, or manicure/pedicure. If you prefer, go out dancing to celebrate life. The intention, not the method, is important. Find whatever heart gateway works for you. It is not about the amount of time you spend in this space; it is about the conscious awareness you bring to the connection.

4. **Experiment with love.** For the next couple of days, conduct an experiment where you dedicate your meditation practice to a particular loved one. This can be any person that you are in a current relationship with (partner, parent, child, sibling or friend). Each day, send loving kindness to that person during your meditation. Whenever you think of the person, visualise them living out their highest potential. Don't tell them that you have chosen them as the focus of your meditation and have no expectation of receiving anything in return. Within 48–72 hours, you can expect to hear from this person. They will reach out to you as they receive your positive energy.

CHAPTER 39

Awareness Practices— Inner Technology to Get Conscious

You are the sky. Everything else—it's just the weather.

PEMA CHODRON, BUDDHIST NUN AND WRITER

☐ There are four practices that are vital in the art of creating conscious awareness: meditation, mindfulness, heartfulness and focusing. These practices are potent 'inner technologies' that rewire our neural pathways and train our consciousness to become more powerful than our automatic, reactive brain. They reduce stress, enhance our cognitive capacity, and make us more hopeful, inspired and connected. They are the stepping stones to experiencing life as the miracle we want it to be.

If used daily, **these practices are guaranteed to positively transform your life.**

Lasting change can only be achieved from **a mental state beyond our thoughts.** This means that we cannot create change from our quick-thinking 'beta' brainwaves. To go beyond our thoughts, we must calm the brain and access the slower alpha, theta and delta brainwaves.

This chapter outlines four scientifically-endorsed methods for silencing (or at least quieting) the 'monkey mind.' Once we go beyond our thoughts, we can enter a state of pure being.

The miracle of meditation

Buddha was asked: *What have you gained from meditation?*
Buddha replied: *Nothing. However, let me tell you what*
                     I have lost: anger, anxiety, depression,
                     insecurity, fear of old age and death.

To start your awareness practice, I suggest that you commit to **at least ten minutes a day** of meditation. Meditation is a way of self-regulating the mind into a particular state of consciousness. There are many varieties of meditation: some are based on the breath; some are based on closing the eyes and repeating a mantra; some are based on concentrating our attention on a particular object; and some are based on focusing on a desired feeling, such as compassion, generosity, kindness or love. All meditations have this in common: they involve an extended period of **focused silence.**

The goal of meditation is to 'bring mental processes under greater voluntary control and thereby foster general mental wellbeing and development, and/or specific capacities such as calm, clarity and concentration' (Walsh & Shapiro, 2006, pp. 228–229). Meditation is the best known way for individuals to single-handedly retrain attention from emotions such as anxiety, depression and anger into 'a subjective experience that is frequently described as very restful, silent, and of heightened alertness, often characterised as blissful' (Jevning et al, 1992).

When we begin to meditate, it is common to feel that we are 'not good at it' or 'unable to do it.' I hear this all the time. I also notice that people often try to meditate when they are at their most stressed (3am and can't sleep; wired on the bus after work; or just after an argument) and then they decide that it doesn't work. Yet training our minds is the same as training our bodies. When we start a new exercise routine, it can take several weeks until we start to feel energised by it, rather than exhausted from it. Exercise doesn't make us feel the same each time, but it generally makes us feel better than we did beforehand. It's the same with meditation.

And just as most people don't feel the full, stabilising effects of antidepressants for six to eight weeks after they start their medication, meditation is a skill that must be practised every day for at least six to eight weeks until we experience its full power. This doesn't mean that it will take that long for meditation to have an effect.

Depending on how it is practised, the beginning of a meditation practice affects people differently. Some people feel the benefits immediately. One client reported that he felt anxious during the first few weeks of meditation, because of the mental clutter that was being cleared away. Some people feel as though they are simply watching an uncomfortable re-run of their lives when meditating, and don't persist with it. For me, my thoughts tend to become more exaggerated at the beginning of meditation, like the volume has been turned up in my mind. This is uncomfortable, particularly when meditation is supposed to quieten the mind! But when I persist, my thoughts start to get quieter and are eventually replaced with a wide, oceanic feeling of peace. It's worth it. I urge you to keep up your practice, regardless of first impressions. If you had a practice that has fallen away, pick it up again. It can be the difference between a good life and a transcendent life.

When do I meditate?

There is no perfect time of the day to meditate, although meditating at certain times of the day offers different benefits. For example, early morning meditations are often recommended, as this practice can offer clarity and focus for the remainder of the day. Yet afternoon meditations can offer reflection and wisdom, and an energy boost into the evening. Meditating before bed can aid sleep quality and also invite vivid or even lucid dreams.

It is up to you to work out the best time for meditation in your life. The most important factor is that your meditation time is sustainable. Try to meditate at the same time each day, so that you establish a pattern. In this course, your meditation will ideally take place in silence and solitude, with your eyes closed. You can be seated or lying down in a comfortable position, with your arms and legs relaxed and uncrossed.

How do I meditate?

While there are many types of meditation, I recommend a very simple breath meditation to beginners. Start by sitting comfortably on the floor, on a chair or lying down on your back. Rest the palms of your hands facing up on your thighs or knees, depending on how you are positioned.

Take a deep breath and feel your heart beating. The breath is the gateway between the mind and the heart. The breath can be calming and enriching, or laboured and shallow. For between ten and twenty minutes each day, focus intently on all aspects of your breath: the rise and fall of your chest, the sound of your inhale and exhale, and the beating of your heart.

Recognise how many millions of processes are happening in your body, as you take each breath. When your mind wanders, silently repeat the words 'thinking, thinking' then return to the breath. Imagine your thoughts passing over your mind like clouds passing through the sky. Watch them float by.

Feel your eyes, jaw and cheeks relax, as you move deeper into your practice. Let your tongue drop to the bottom of your mouth, as your mental activity loses its intensity. With each breath, your neck and shoulders become soft. Your breath starts to sound and feel like the rhythm of the ocean, with the inhale representing the receding flow and the exhale representing waves crashing onto the shore.

In the early stages, you may fall asleep during meditation, or you may feel like you are replaying a movie of your recent past in your head. Meditation is an excavation process that allows us to clear out mental residue. Your key task is simply to meditate daily. Science guarantees that your mind will transform.

Note: It can be helpful to start with a guided meditation, especially if you're meditating on the go. There are guided meditations available on my website: www.drawalker.com

The flow of mindfulness

While meditation is intensely-focused time in silence, mindfulness or 'conscious flow' can be practised throughout the day. Mindfulness is a particular mental state, where we focus our awareness entirely on the present, while calmly acknowledging and accepting any transient feelings, thoughts and bodily sensations that arise. There are many studies that report the benefits of mindfulness. It has been found to reduce stress, boost memory, improve focus, reduce emotional reactivity, increase cognitive flexibility and heighten relationship satisfaction. Mindfulness has also been shown to transform self-insight, morality, intuition and fear modulation. For references and more information on all of these studies, see Davis and Hayes, 2011.

Mindfulness is for everyone. A good friend of mine is a very distractive and animated person. It is hard to imagine him sitting still or being quiet. He said to me once, 'You know I never understood you carrying on about mindfulness until I went snowboarding recently. I was completely in the moment the whole time, from the top of the hill until the end. It was amazing. I didn't realise that you could be mindful in the middle of anything.'

Mindfulness is similar to the 'flow state,' described by Csikszentmihalyi as a mental state in which a person is fully absorbed in a feeling of focus, involvement and enjoyment during an activity (1990). It is used as a therapeutic technique, because our stress and unhappiness always come from either anticipating the future or dwelling on the past. Mindfulness is a witness to every moment of our life, from the mundane to the magnificent. It is the non-judgemental, bird's-eye view we have of our life, at the same time as we are living it. The more we are able to inhabit this internal watcher or observer, the more aware we become. Mindfulness can only arise when we surrender the need for our brain to control every detail of our life.

Mindfulness can be brought into every moment of the day: while driving, working, walking and relating. When you are eating, taste each bite and savour the flavours. Think of all the people who made your meal possible. While you are showering, cleaning your teeth, applying make-up, shaving, brushing your hair or getting dressed, just breathe and be in the moment. If you are on your way somewhere, be fully in the car, bus or train. In a conversation with anyone, focus only on that mental space. Focus all of your attention on the sensations you have in every moment. Bring all of yourself into the present. Hear the sounds.

Dedicate time each day away from technology and screens, with no computer, TV or phone within reach. Just enjoy the quiet time in 'low stimulation.' This is particularly important for children and young adults, whose brains are still developing. Read a book, have a conversation, colour in a mindful colouring book, sculpt clay, paint, potter in the garden, or play music and disconnect from the constant hum, while staying focused on your breathing. Even if you are at the shops or taking your children to the park, stay absorbed in the present moment. These practices bring a new quality of mindful attention to your life. It makes a distinction between the thinker in our outer world and the shaper of our inner world.

When we are deeply attuned to the power of focused awareness, we seek out mindfulness as often as possible. We are less distracted by the lower levels of reactive attention. We do not spend a large amount of time in hyper-stimulated mental states that preoccupy our mind with chatter. We live our life from a place of reflection and observation. **It is life-changing to watch your thoughts and be curious about them, instead of identifying with them.** Mindfulness is a state of mind that allows us to bring awareness to all of our experiences, regardless of their magnitude. Although we might look the same on the outside, we are filled with a deep appreciation for each moment on the inside.

When we start the day, we eat mindfully and express silent gratitude for those who made our meal possible. This small act sends positive messages to our brain, boosting our capacity to notice joy and happiness. Then we have a shower, feeling the water on our back, practising deep breathing. We get dressed for the day ahead, acknowledging the miracle of our bodies and brains that allow us to participate in life. We do not have background recordings constantly playing in our mind of the past and future. We turn the volume down on the lower levels of consciousness and we turn up the experience of mindfulness. We allow the world to meet us halfway. Without our judgements and attachments, life simply becomes a series of moments happening in front of us.

Mindfulness is possible even with children running around or with deadlines looming. When life does not go according to plan and we spend the day cleaning spilt milk off the floor, or we miss the bus, or we don't feel well, or we are comforting a crying child, or we are sitting in traffic, or we are running around the house looking for one last pair of clean socks . . . we can still bring our full awareness to those moments. Mindfulness is a state of mind that can be practised anytime and anywhere; it is not dependent on a peaceful and perfect environment.

In fact, bringing mindfulness to our life experience makes us better parents, better partners and better workers. We are able to be absorbed in the present moment, which is the greatest gift we can give to the people around us. When we practise mindfulness, it is as though our daily tasks practically complete themselves.

In the song *A Spoonful of Sugar* from *Mary Poppins*, the characters use mindfulness to bring excitement to mundane tasks. Mary Poppins brings joy and awareness to the present moment by singing:

In every job that must be done, there is an element of fun.
You find the fun, and snap! The job's a game.
And every task you undertake becomes a piece of cake,
A lark, a spree, it's very clear to see . . .

After seeing that the present moment is all we ever have, we surrender to it. Then it seems as if the jobs we have to complete happen by magic.

Once we are able to master mindfulness in our day-to-day routines, this practice creates a ripple effect in our interpersonal interactions. We are able to participate in mindful conversations, where we give others our full presence and attention. We listen intently to what others are saying, rather than simply waiting to speak. At work, rather than distributing our focus across ten different tasks, we are able to focus on one task without our brain constantly urging us to check our email, scroll through social media feeds, or make a phone call. We gain attentional control over our brain. In the midst of conflict, we find ourselves able to bring mindfulness to our thoughts and feelings.

The first time this happened to me, I was shocked—it was like the argument was happening in slow motion. Rather than blurting out the first defensive words that came to mind, I was able to bring mindfulness to the dispute, looking for a higher perspective to resolve the conflict. And I acknowledged my role in it much sooner, which would normally have taken me hours or days to do.

Living love: heartfulness

When we bring mindfulness to our interpersonal connections, they take on a new dimension: heartfulness.

Dancing with dear friends under the moonlight. Talking for hours in front of an open fire. Diving into the clear, blue ocean. Watching a sunset. Singing harmonies. Flying overseas for the first time. Flying overseas for the first time alone, and feeling the plane leave the ground. Surprising my family by coming home for Christmas. Getting engaged. Hearing my favourite song on the radio. Walking down the aisle with my dad on my wedding day. Finding out that I am pregnant. Seeing the faces of my babies. Zooming past rice paddies in Bali on a motorbike with my husband. Hearing my children laugh. Feeling that my heart might explode out of my chest. This is heartfulness in me. My joy, my ecstasy . . . the punctuation marks of my life.

Heartfulness occurs when our moment-to-moment awareness expands to encompass emotions of joy, compassion and interconnectedness with all other living beings. Heartfulness is the feeling of our cup running over with gratitude for all of life. It arises when we learn to go with the flow of life and act from a place of self-love. We feel ecstatic. We access pure being.

Heartfulness communicates in goosebumps, tears of joy and a passionate, racing heart.

Heartfulness often surfaces during a reflective practice with others. I feel 'heartful' at the end of a yoga class when we all chant Om together. The resonant sounds of our voices lifted together makes me feel as though we are one being, inextricably connected for one moment in time. I feel the same during a group meditation practice, whether I am a participant or the facilitator. Our collective thinking subsides and is replaced with a union of collective feelings: hearts joined as one.

Heartfulness is the gift of existence—pure awareness that unites our mind and body in the present moment and connects us to all of life.

Heartfulness is the sudden sense of transcendence that may come during exposure to a particular piece of music or art, a deep meditation, intense feelings of love or in the midst of majestic nature. Abraham Maslow called these transcendent moments 'peak experiences'. He described them as naturally-induced moments of intense joy, euphoria and inspiration, which leave us renewed and transformed (1964). A peak experience might happen while sipping tea in front of a log fire. It might happen while watching the sunrise, with your baby sleeping peacefully in your arms. It might happen during an orgasm. It might happen at the top of a mountain you have just climbed, while you are singing in the car, or in a yoga class on the beach.

In these moments, we often feel inspired to channel our emotion through some form of creative expression, such as writing, dancing, painting, poetry, sculpting or playing music. We do not want to lose the feeling. We want it recorded in some way for all time, because we know that these experiences are the best that life can offer. Heartfulness evokes tears of joy and shivers down the spine. The most intense peak experiences include: 'feelings of limitless horizons opening up to the vision, the feeling of being simultaneously more powerful and more helpless than one ever was before, the feeling of great ecstasy and wonder and awe, and the loss of placing in time and space' (Maslow, 1964, p. 164).

Peak experiences allow us to connect with the deeper meaning and value of our existence.

Heartfulness is consciousness at its most beautiful and transcendent. It is the lover's territory, where it is free to be anything it desires. It may spontaneously dive into the water, sing in the shower, hug a loved one, dance around the room, laugh out loud, or serenely sit on the grass. Here, the lover is not simply mindful in the present moment, **the lover relishes every moment.** The world stops and our lover is carried away with inspiration. The lover is colourful, affectionate and ardent. The lover transforms into a lover of life, savouring every bite, every kiss, every breeze and every song.

In a state of heartfulness, we are able to experience everyday ecstasy.

The dedicated practices of meditation and mindfulness prime our brains for heartfulness, which operates on gamma brainwaves. Gamma waves are the highest, fastest frequency of all the brainwaves. In a gamma state, our brains create patterns of conscious flow, harmony and coherence. This was shown in a 2004 study of Tibetan monks. The study involved eight long-term Tibetan Buddhist meditators, who underwent mental training in the same Tibetan Nyingmapa and Kagyupa traditions for 10,000 to 50,000 hours, over time periods ranging from fifteen to forty years. The study used electrodes to monitor the activity produced by their brains as they meditated.

The researchers then compared the brain activity of the monks to a group of beginner meditators. This group was made up of ten healthy student volunteers, all around 21 years of age. They had no previous meditative experience, but had declared an interest in meditation. They underwent meditative training for one week before the collection of the data.

In a normal meditative state, both groups had similar brain activity. This is fantastic news for all beginner meditators! However, something magical happened when the monks were directed to generate a feeling of unconditional loving kindness and pure compassion during their meditation. This was described as an 'unrestricted readiness and availability to help living beings.' The monks' brain activity was unexpected and brilliant. It began to fire in a rhythmic, harmonious way, at a frequency of 25–40 Hz (gamma waves). These gamma oscillations in the monks' brain signals were the largest ever recorded in healthy humans. The monks' training and experience with meditation allowed their brain to function at the highest level of pure coherence. There was little to no resistance in the brains of the monks to the feelings of heartfulness.

Achieving gamma brainwaves may explain the feelings of bliss and higher consciousness that we experience after meditation. The same waves were scarce in the beginner meditators, however they strengthened as the beginners had more experience with the exercise. This tells us that achieving gamma brainwaves can be trained. (Lutz et al., 2004).

So we can see that heartfulness is the combination of mindful absorption in the moment and a conscious feeling of loving kindness and compassion. Heartfulness exists on the frequency of gamma brainwaves. Most of us feel heartful every now and then, but we know that heartfulness, like mindfulness and meditation, can be trained and is the result of daily practice.

The ocean and the sky: an awareness practice

Try this simple exercise to practise mindfulness and heartfulness. Start by taking a deep breath in and out, and tune into your immediate environment. Bring your mind into the present moment.

Step 1: Amplify your senses

For example, you may hear the breeze blowing through the trees, the sounds of distant construction, an aeroplane flying overhead or a pottering neighbour. You may hear birds chirping, a siren or a dog barking. You may smell wafting aromatic tea, a candle or freshly-washed hair. You read the words in this book and your peripheral vision is aware of the place you are in, perhaps a window or a door. Your hands are holding the book or the device on which you are reading these words. Feel it in your hands. Be absorbed in your senses. Take another breath.

Step 2: Notice your background thoughts

I need to leave in an hour. I should get ready. I wonder what the traffic will be like. What will I wear? I need to send that email. I might have another coffee. What are we having for dinner tonight?

Step 3: Notice your background feelings

I'm excited about my holiday. I feel drained all the time. I feel like I'm letting everyone down. I'm inspired to learn something new. Rather than identifying with these feelings, simply notice them. These senses, thoughts and feelings are your body/brain machine working overtime. When you are awake, your body/brain machine is never off. The only thing you can do is to bring mindfulness to the machine. Take another deep breath in and out.

Step 4: Mindfulness

Now, become the observer who is watching your thoughts, feelings and senses. The observer is objective and calm. The observer is not attached to thoughts and emotions. The observer is like the sky over the ocean. The sky does not get pulled into the tides. The sky is not swept away by the wind. The sky is not overpowered by the sun. For a few minutes, become the watcher of your life. Imagine you are pulled into the sky, looking down on your life. Become the sky over the waves of your thoughts and feelings. Inhabit the expansive higher perspective. Take another deep breath in and out.

Step 5: Heartfulness

Now, feel the calm wash over you. Feel your connection to all other beings. Allow the power of your heart to radiate out and touch all that cross your path. Extend loving kindness to your loved ones, and then to all people, animals and the earth. Bring your hands together in a prayer position. Lift your hands to your forehead and say: *Right thoughts*. Place your hands on your lips and say: *Right words*. Finish with your hands in a prayer position over your heart and say: *Right action*.

Finish the exercise with a deep inhale and exhale.

The focusing technique: enter consciousness

The final practice that I want to share with you is **focusing**. It is my favourite daily technique for awareness and has been empirically proven to have transformative effects. It was developed by psychotherapist and philosopher Eugene Gendlin at the University of Chicago in 1978. (For more information, see his book *Focusing* [1981]). Gendlin carried out research over fifteen years on the success of psychotherapy. He discovered that patients who have the best outcomes are the ones who are able to engage with their inner wisdom and intuitive felt sense (what I would call their consciousness). He created a technique to facilitate this connection called 'focusing'.

Focusing can be used whenever we need to connect with our inner wisdom: when we are feeling indecisive, uninspired, anxious, upset, depressed, or when we can't relax. It can also be used to access joy and peace. Here are the steps:

Step 1: Tune into your body

For most people, this usually happens in solitude, in a quiet space, sitting or lying down. When you get used to the process, you can practise focusing anywhere. I now occasionally practise focusing while I'm in the car!

Step 2: Ask yourself

Where do I feel this emotion or discomfort (eg. indecision, restlessness, anxiety, or depression) in my body? Where is this sensation located?

Step 3: Wait for your body to show you the answer

Don't block it; don't judge it; don't resist. Many people give up here and think: *I can't do this. I can't feel anything.* Be patient. Something will arise and ask for your attention. You will get what is called a 'felt sense.' You will feel a dominant sensation somewhere in your body that is a response to you tuning in. It may come in the form of a feeling, such as a tingling in your fingers or an ache in your neck. It may come in the form of an image. It might be butterflies in your stomach, a vice around your neck or daggers in your back. This is your body communicating a symbol to you that represents the discomfort. It might also shift as you bring awareness to it—just follow it.

Let it go wherever it needs to go and let it transform into what it needs to become. For example, butterflies might turn into fire, then into a snake and then into a spaceship. You need to get really clear on this felt sense—the clearer the better. Describe it to yourself in as much detail as possible. It may stay the same the whole time, but it will eventually settle into something. Once you have settled on the sensation or the image, you have found your felt sense. Once you are clear on your felt sense, take the next transformative step.

Step 4: Ask the felt sense what it's like from its point of view

Ask the butterflies what they're feeling; ask the vice what it's like; and ask the daggers about their perspective. You are attempting to uncover their role in your process. Why is this discomfort showing up for you? What is the message behind the pain? What does this pain represent for your growth and awareness? This is the moment that you access your consciousness through the wisdom of your body.

Again, be patient, open and receptive. Don't resist it because you feel inhibited. Just trust the process—it will work if you persist. The answer may come in the form of a new image or an emotion or a clear thought. You just know what the answer is. If you can't feel it, stay with it. Stay connected to the felt sense. It will communicate with you.

Step 5: Ask the felt sense what it wants and needs to be healed

This is a powerful and often surprising process. The answer you receive might be simple, for example: *I need to get some rest. I'm under too much pressure—I just can't go out tonight.* Or, *I don't feel comfortable taking on that new client; I don't have a good feeling about them.*

The answer could also be life changing: *I need to leave this relationship; it is not aligned with my highest good.* Or, *I need to transform my lifestyle. I can't keep eating/drinking like this. It's toxic and destroying my body.*

Focusing allows us to tap into our intuitive wisdom. The art of focusing allows us to bypass our thoughts and communicate directly with our emotions and senses. It is a practical healing and empowerment tool that can be used at any time by anyone. I hope it is as powerful for you as it has been for me.

After your first experiment with focusing, draw the images that came to you and track how they unfolded. This is a powerful way for your consciousness to communicate with you.

Once we dedicate ourselves to a daily practice of being, we can expect to regularly experience:

- ☐ Transcendent states of consciousness, such as deep relaxation and inner peace; and
- ☐ Peak experiences: naturally induced moments of intense joy, ecstasy and inspiration, which leave us renewed and transformed (Maslow, 1964).

There are other miraculous awareness practices that are based on the same themes. Practices such as yoga, tai chi and qigong all incorporate the breath and movement and have the same effects as the practices I have mentioned. Once you find a practice you love, the key is practising as often as possible.

Being

The being experiences everyday ecstasy through peak experiences. The being enters a state of mindfulness, heartfulness, intuition, collective consciousness, unity, and interconnectedness with all of life.

unconditional love, generosity of spirit, ecstasy, trust, abundance, kindness, compassion

Affirmations for being:

☐ *I experience everyday ecstasy.*
☐ *I am one with the flow of life.*
☐ *I am love.*

Write these affirmations down and put them in a prominent place where you will see them every day (beside your bed, on your desk or on the fridge). Say them aloud to yourself every night.

POSES

Lotus pose and savasana (use these poses to experience everyday ecstasy, as you deepen your meditation practice).

Reflecting on our actions

☐ The key to acting with conscious awareness is to surrender to the present moment.
☐ We do this by asking: *What needs to be expressed through me?* and *Who needs me to be a part of their purpose?*
☐ Any lasting change can only happen when we access brainwaves that are slower than our thinking 'monkey mind'.
☐ To slow down the mind, we need a daily practice of meditation, mindfulness, heartfulness and focusing.

REFLECTIONS

CHAPTER 40

The Hall of Mirrors

☐ Imagine that you are walking down a long hallway with doors on either side. Each door has mirrored panels, so you see yourself in the mirrors as you pass. All of the doors are shut, and some have handles.

You choose a door with a handle and open it, just a little. As you glance around behind the door, you witness a royal scene. You are looking into the front lawn of a palace. You take a step through the door into the palace grounds. As you look around, everyone notices you and falls silent. Suddenly people begin to bow before you and you are ushered towards your throne. As you sit, a crown is placed reverently upon your head. You feel noble and powerful.

You are suddenly whooshed back into the hallway. You open the next door handle and look behind the door. You see a verdant green valley and a lush paddock, with a majestic white horse sitting down, waiting for you to climb on. Your gear and saddle are ready for you on the horse, so all you need to do is jump on and start your ride. Without hesitating you walk over, take your seat on the horse and set off. You have never felt freer. You breathe deeply and smile.

Again you are back in the hallway. You see another door and open it slightly. It is a large meditation room in a monastery. There are one hundred monks all seated, silently meditating. They don't notice you, or if they do, they do not react. You take your seat beside another monk, close your eyes and take a deep breath. Your breathing settles into a calming rhythm and the atmosphere in the room is hypnotic. Within minutes, you enter a void of bliss.

You are once again back in the hallway. The next door you come to is locked. It has chains over it and a huge padlock. It has graffiti scrawled over it and you read the words 'Do Not Enter.' You shrug and keep walking. Why would you bother with this door, when all of the other doors bring such happiness?

The next door is unlocked. You peer around it and you are suddenly staggering around on a ship in a storm. You reach out for some support and there is nothing. You fall and slide down the deck as a wave turns the vessel on its side. The ship rights itself, almost defying gravity, and you find a mast to cling onto. Your shipmates are sliding around trying to tie knots and secure ropes, while the captain attempts to steer the ship out of the storm. You feel exhilarated, but you fear for your life. In one great surge, you lose your grip on the mast and start to fall overboard when . . .

You are once again back in the hallway. As you keep walking, you notice that every door you pass is locked. You continue down the hall, when suddenly all the mirrors turn black and you see white arrows on them, pointing back to the padlocked door. You shrug, then make your way back to that door. All of the other doors have been so exciting and thrilling that this one can't be so bad. You grab at the chains and they suddenly turn to paper in your hands. You pull the paper chains away and drop them on the floor. You touch the padlock. Startled, you pull your hands away and step back. It has given you an electric shock. You are immediately overcome by a feeling of dread and sadness. The door speaks to you: *You don't want to come in here. You hate it in here. We agreed that you would lock this away forever.* You nod. You don't want to feel that way—why would you, when you can be regal, free, blissful and exhilarated?

You move away from the door and start walking down the hallway again. The doors are all locked and many now have chains and a padlock. All of the doors are still black, but one has a light. You walk towards the light and look into the mirror. You see your reflection and you have a thousand faces. Some are radiant, others are smiling, and some are hideous. You slump down on the floor. You decide to stay there for a while. It's easier than dealing with the black and painful doors.

Time passes and you are still sitting in the hallway. You are just in a holding pattern, on automatic pilot, mindlessly waiting for something in the hallway to change.

The hallway never changes, but gradually you do. One day you have a realisation.

The first doors you opened brought you exhilaration, bliss and freedom. All of these doors represented your early life, when everything was new. You experienced things for the first time; you were young and carefree. The world was open to you, in all its radiance and potential. You were invincible and anything was possible. This was a symbol of your childhood.

After you encountered a few obstacles and you began to understand the complexity of life, you began to store your fears and negative beliefs in secret compartments, behind their own doorways. Over time, you built chains and padlocks around them. You thought you were protecting yourself, but you were actually cutting yourself off from all the other doors that would lead you to a sense of purpose, connection and love. Your fears became your obstacles. You started pretending that you were never associated with those doors in the first place.

You recognise that this is a symbol of your mind. The hallway represents your feelings, offering infinite opportunities, depending on the emotions you choose to honour. If you choose to honour and believe in fear and scarcity, more and more doors are closed to you. If you choose to honour and believe in abundance and love, each door beckons with opportunity.

The doorways that you choose to open are your habitual thoughts, with different experiences behind each one. The characters you become when you open the doors are your inner selves: the royal personage in the palace, the freedom-seeking horse rider, the meditator and the sailor. When you reach out and embrace the doors in the hallway, they create physical sensations in your body. The scenes behind the doors are your actions in the world.

You (the self in the hallway) are the consciousness/being/ awareness, constantly choosing where to place your focus and attention; making decisions that actively shape your reality in each moment.

You try an experiment to enter your conscious awareness. You close your eyes and take some deep breaths. You continue to focus on your breath for several minutes, and eventually you relax into a sphere that is separate from your brain and automatic thinking. You become immersed in a feeling of flow, going with the rhythm of the moment. You surrender to this flow.

As you inhabit this new world, you realise that flowing in the moment is just a choice. In the flow of the moment, you can release the need for pressure and control. The flow is pure, relaxed, spontaneous and light. It is music and nature. In the flow, you instinctively know how to love and how to be happy.

When you open your eyes, the locks and chains start falling away from the doors. They all start to gleam and shine in response to the new perspective you are offering. You continue to nudge your mind in the direction of breath awareness, and surrender to the flow of the moment. One by one, the doors open and invite you in. Each breath opens a new door, and each door shapes your experience.

Suddenly you see . . . you were creating your reality all along.

CHAPTER 41

Pure Consciousness— We Are One

☐ The final homecoming, the goal of existence, is the awareness that we are all one. This awareness allows us to inhabit the anima mundi: the being or soul of the world. As David Tacey writes:

> The soul is sick when it does not understand its meaning, that is, when it does not feel connected to the soul of the world, the anima mundi. Without the experience of transcendence, on a regular basis, the soul becomes sick of itself and tired of the world, because it is 'not of this world' but a fragment of a larger divine nature. (2006, p. 90).

Oneness means that our actions, no matter how small, have flow-on effects that we cannot control or predict. Life is a paradox, because we are all-powerful yet dependent, influential yet small, worthy yet humble, and one yet many.

In our appreciation of oneness, we **tread lightly on the earth**. We are aware that each of our actions and interactions has an effect on others. We acknowledge our fundamental connection with every other living being on the planet. The person next door, or on the other side of the world, is a part of me. The animals are a part of me. The trees are a part of me. The oceans are a part of me. We are all connected by consciousness. Oneness consciousness exists in the realm of the unseen. We go beyond our surface, real world reality into infinite connectedness.

Human beings are programmed to evolve and, at this time in our history, evolution allows us to thrive rather than just survive. Evolution used to mean learning to stay alive in the wild, or living beyond the age of forty. It now means evolving the self to a higher level of consciousness. We all have an in-built longing to connect with our consciousness, because this is what ultimately brings us true fulfilment.

Wherever you are, start there and start now. Whatever you can do right now, do that. Now is the perfect time to walk the conscious path. This is about taking small steps in a new direction. This will be the most important voyage of your life, opening into your inner world.

So what are you here to do? The answer to this question brings purpose, power, peace, love, passion and happiness. The answer for every living being in the universe is the same: **I am here to get conscious.**

References and Further Reading

Altschuler, E.L. & Ramachandran, V.S. (2007) 'A simple method to stand outside oneself', *Perception*, vol. 36(4), pp. 632–4.

Antony, M. (2001) 'Is Consciousness Ambiguous?' *Journal of Consciousness Studies*, vol. 8, pp. 19–44.

Blackmore, S. (2003) *Consciousness: An Introduction*, London: Hodder & Stoughton.

Block, N. (1998) 'On a Confusion About a Function of Consciousness,' in N. Block, O. Flanagan & G. Guzeldere, *The Nature of Consciousness: Philosophical Debates*, Boston: MIT Press.

Boorstein, S. (2008) *Happiness is an Inside Job: Practicing for a Joyful Life*, New York: Random House.

Brown, B. (2010) *The Gifts of Imperfection: Let Go of Who You Think You're Supposed to be and Embrace Who You Are*, Center City, Minnesota: Hazelden.

Casement, A. (2006) 'The Shadow,' in Papadopoulos, Renos (ed.) *The Handbook of Jungian Psychology: Theory, Practice & Applications*, Hove: Routledge.

Chalmers, D. (1995) 'Facing up to the Problem of Consciousness,' *Journal of Consciousness Studies*, vol. 2, pp. 200–219.

Csikszentmihalyi, M. (1990) *Flow: The Psychology of Happiness*, New York: Harper & Row.

Davis, D. and Hayes, J. (2011) 'What are the Benefits of Mindfulness? A Practice Review of Psychotherapy-Related Research,' *Psychotherapy*, vol. 48(2), pp. 198–208.

Doidge, N. (2008) *The Brain that Changes Itself*, Melbourne: Scribe Publications.

Dweck, S. (2006) *Mindset: The New Psychology of Success*, New York: Random House.

Fowler, J.H. & Christakis, N.A. (2008) 'Dynamic spread of happiness in a large social network: longitudinal analysis over 20 years in the Framingham Heart Study,' *BMJ* 2008; 337: a2338: http://www.bmj.com/content/337/bmj.a2338.long

Gendlin, E. (1981) *Focusing* (2nd ed.) New York: Bantam Books.

Greene, B. (2011) *The Hidden Reality: Parallel Universes and the Deep Laws of the Cosmos*, New York: Alfred A. Knopf.

Greenfield, S. (2002) 'Mind, Brain & Consciousness,' *The British Journal of Psychiatry*, vol. 181, pp. 91–93.

Jevning, R. Wallace, R.K & Beidebach, M. (1992). 'The Physiology of Meditation: A Review: A Wakeful Hypometabolic Integrated Response,' *Neuroscience & Biobehavioral Reviews*, vol. 16(3), pp. 415–424.

Jung, C. (2001) [1933] *Modern Man in Search of a Soul*, Abingdon: Routledge.

Jung, C.G. (1964) [1918] Collected Works of C.G. Jung, Volume Ten: Civilization in Transition, (ed and trans. Gerhard Adler and R.F.C. Hull), London: Routledge and Kegan Paul.

Kandel, E.R., Schwartz, J.H. & Jessell, T.M. (2000) *Principles of Neural Science*, New York: McGraw-Hill.

Ketola, T. (2008) 'Taming the Shadow: Corporate Responsibility in a Jungian Context,' *Corporate Social Responsibility and Environmental Management*, vol. 15(4), pp. 199–209.

Lajoie, D. H. & Shapiro, S. (1992) 'Definitions of Transpersonal Psychology: The First Twenty-Three Years,' *Journal of Transpersonal Psychology*, vol. 24(1), pp. 79–98.

Lane, A. M., Beedie, C. J., Jones, M. V., Uphill, M. & Devonport, T. J. (2012) 'The BASES Expert Statement on Emotion Regulation in Sport,' *Journal of Sports Science*, vol. 30, pp. 1189–1195.

Langer, E. J. (2009) *Counter Clockwise: Mindful Health and the Power of Possibility*, New York: Ballantine Books.

Lutz, A., Greischar, L.L., Rawlings, N.B., Ricard M. & Davidson, R.J. (2004) 'Long-term meditators self-induce high amplitude gamma synchrony during mental practice,' *Proceedings of the National Academy of Sciences USA*, vol. 101, pp. 16369–16373.

Lycan, W. (1996) *Consciousness and Experience*, Boston: MIT Press.

Main, R. (2006) in Papadopoulos, Renos (ed.) *The Handbook of Jungian Psychology: Theory, Practice and Applications*, Hove: Routledge.

Maslow, A. (1964) *Religions, Values and Peak Experiences*, New York: Viking Press.

Moores, D. (2005) 'Young Goodman Brown's "Evil Purpose": Hawthorne and the Jungian Shadow,' *Journal of Evolutionary Psychology*, vol. 27 (3/4, October), pp. 4–17.

Oberman, L.M. & Ramachandran, V.S. (2007) 'The simulating social mind: the role of the mirror neuron system and simulation in the social and communicative deficits of autism spectrum disorders,' *Psychological Bulletin*, vol. 133(2), pp. 310–27.

Ramachandran, V.S. & Rogers-Ramachandran, D. (2007) 'It's All Done with Mirrors,' *Scientific American Mind*, vol. 18(4), pp. 16–18.

Ramachandran, V.S. (2011) *The Tell-Tale Brain: A Neuroscientist's Quest for What Makes Us Human*, New York: W. W. Norton & Company.

Ramachandran, V.S. (2004) *A Brief Tour of Human Consciousness: From Impostor Poodles to Purple Numbers*, New York: Pi Press.

Richardson, A. (1969) Mental Imagery, New York: Springer.

Rifkin, J. (2010) *The Empathic Civilization: The Race to Global Consciousness in a World in Crisis*, New York: Penguin.

Seligman, M. (2004) *Authentic Happiness: Using the New Positive Psychology to Realize Your Potential for Lasting Fulfillment*, New York: Atria Books.

Stevens, A. (2006) 'The Archetypes' in Papadopoulos, Renos (ed.) *The Handbook of Jungian Psychology: Theory, Practice & Applications*, Hove: Routledge.

Stone, H. & Stone, S. (1989) *Embracing Our Selves: The Voice Dialogue Manual*, Novato: New World Library.

Tacey, D. (2006) How to Read Jung, London: Granta Books. Tassi, P. & Muzet, A. (2001) 'Defining the States of Consciousness,' *Neuroscience & Behavioral Reviews* (March), 25(2), pp. 175–191.

Tolle, E. (2005) *A New Earth*, New York: Dutton/Penguin Group.

Velmans, M. & Schneider, S. (eds.) (2006) *The Blackwell Companion to Consciousness*, Malden: Blackwell.

Walsh, R. & Shapiro, S. (2006) 'The Meeting of Meditative Disciplines and Western Psychology: A Mutually Enriching Dialogue,' *American Psychologist*, vol. 61(3), pp. 227–229.

Walsh, R. & Vaughan, F. (1993) *Paths Beyond Ego: The Transpersonal Vision*, New York: Jeremy P. Tarcher.

Weiser Cornell, A. (1996) *The Power of Focusing: A Practical Guide to Emotional Self-Healing,* Oakland: New Harbinger.

Wendt, A. (2010) 'Flatland: Quantum Mind and the International Hologram', Chapter 11 in Albert, M., Cederman, L. & Wendt, A. (eds) *New Systems Theories of World Politics*, Palgrave Studies in International Relations, Basingstoke: Palgrave Macmillan.

Yapko, M. (2009) *Depression is Contagious: How the Most Common Mood Disorder Is Spreading Around the World and How to Stop It,* New York: Free Press.

Young-Eisendrath, P. & Dawson, T. (eds.) (1997) *The Cambridge Companion to Jung,* Cambridge: Cambridge University Press.

Acknowledgements

☐ This book has been over ten years in the making. When I was in my early twenties, I would go for long walks and drives listening to audio books of Hay House authors, particularly Caroline Myss and Wayne Dyer. To have my first book published by Hay House Australia is a dream come true, and I thank them for seeing a spark of creation in me. I particularly want to thank Leon Nacson and Rosie Barry for their guidance and support.

To Mum and Dad, thank you for inspiring my love of life and learning. Thank you for believing in me and showing me the way. You are both angels on earth, and I am lucky and ever grateful to be your daughter. I am who I am because of you. Mum, I can't even count the hours we have spent talking about the things I end up writing about. You are a muse to so many! My work is a testament to your wisdom, love and commitment.

To my brothers, Paul and David, and my sisters, Bridget and Isabelle—I'm not me without you. I love you all intensely. To my aunty, Mary Machatsch, you are an original inspiration and have always been a heroine to me. To my sister-in-law,

Claudia Walker, thank you for your friendship, love, infectious optimism and invaluable feedback on the draft.

To my parents-in-law, Jenny and Bill, and sisters-in-law Sophie, Anna and Claudia, thank you for your generosity, humour and open hearts. Thank you for welcoming me into your family. Jenny, I wrote so much of this book while you looked after Raph—thank you!

To all of my many dear friends and teachers, I am forever grateful for your companionship, conversations and guidance— you know who you are! Thank you particularly to Henrietta Rowe, Patrice Corrie, Jacqui Scruby, Arianne Sweeting, Angela Cummine, Sally Ioannides, Alissa Warren, Ellen Slaven, Alice Finn, Abbey Bertuca and Laura Brennan. To my neighbours, Dianna Lee, Helen Cook and Olivia Cook—your support means more to me than you will ever know.

To Raphael and Theodore: you are too young to read this, but you have already taught me more than I could learn in a lifetime without you. I love you. Al, our family . . . our love . . . is the light of my life.

ABOUT THE AUTHOR

Ali Walker PhD is a social researcher and lecturer at the Centre for Social Impact, UNSW Sydney. Her work focuses on the question: *What conditions lead to personal and social flourishing?*

Ali spent several years researching consciousness, social change and law with a doctorate from the Australian National University. In addition to her PhD, Ali has a Masters degree in International Law and International Relations and two undergraduate degrees in Law and Arts from UNSW Sydney. She lives in Sydney with her husband and two sons.

www.drawalker.com

221

HAY HOUSE

Look within

Join the conversation about latest products,
events, exclusive offers and more.

 Hay House UK

 @HayHouseUK

 @hayhouseuk

 healyourlife.com

We'd love to hear from you!